How to Change Your Life

Self-help Books

Susan Kersley

Published by Susan Kersley, 2023.

While every precaution has been taken in the preparation of this book, the publisher assumes no responsibility for errors or omissions, or for damages resulting from the use of the information contained herein.

HOW TO CHANGE YOUR LIFE

First edition. December 10, 2023.

ISBN: 979-8223882725

Written by Susan Kersley.

Table of Contents

How to Change Your Life

Susan Kersley

18. Be more efficient.

19. Set a time limit for each task.

20. Take regular breaks.

21. Work with a deadline.

22. Get help from others.

23. Delegate more effectively

24. Clear your desk completely.

25. Throw away lots.

26. Keep accounts up to date.

27. Spend less time on the Internet.

28. Check emails only twice a day.

Part 3: Decision Making

29. Gain Clarity.

30. Group your choices together.

31. Chunk down your choice.

32. Make a list of pros and cons.

33. Notice your internal voice.

34. Notice Your Gut Feelings

35. Consider alternatives.

36. Prepare for all eventualities.

Introduction

Overcoming life challenges requires adjustments, even if the solution seems obvious. The most important thing to do is to make a start, however small. When you take the first step, the next steps become much easier.

Strange though it may seem, when you change any part of your life, other changes become easier.

Even simple changes, for example to your hairstyle or clothing, can lead to bigger changes.

This book offers you a multitude of ways to change your life. Pick those that resonate with you and be open to transforming your life.

PART ONE: Work-Life Balance

Work-life balance refers to the proper division of time and energy between one's job or career and one's personal life and responsibilities. It involves finding the right balance between work-related commitments and obligations, such as meeting deadlines, attending meetings, or completing projects, and personal activities, such as spending time with family and friends, pursuing hobbies and interests, or taking care of one's well-being.

It includes the ability to prioritise and manage one's time effectively to maintain physical and mental well-being and satisfaction in different areas of life.

Achieving work-life balance can lead to reduced stress, improved productivity, and enhanced overall quality of life.

1. Set SMART goals.

———

Setting SMART goals is essential to achieving success. Whether for personal growth, career advancement, or daily tasks, goals increase your motivation. Knowing what you want makes you more likely to succeed. Don't be vague, instead define precisely what you want and by when. If your goal is, for example, 'I want to be happier,' define what that means to you. Your goals must be specific and measurable. Vague goals such as "I want to be successful" lack clarity. Setting specific goals, such as walking for 30 minutes daily, helps you track progress better than indefinable goals.

SMART goals give you a sense of purpose and direction, helping you to stay focused and motivated. Unclear intentions lead to confusion and lack of incentive, making it difficult to decide what to do and to measure your progress.

Break down large goals into smaller aims, and create a simple action plan. This enables you to make progress towards your desired outcome. When you split a big goal into small steps, you can track your progress more easily and celebrate each achievement as you go. Using this approach prevents overwhelm and you stay motivated.

Your goals should be achievable and realistic. While it is essential to dream big, setting unrealistic goals can lead to frustration and disappointment. Realistic goals motivate you and are the key to supporting your motivation and progress.

Decide the time by when you want to achieve your goal. A goal without a timeframe lacks a sense of urgency and often leads to procrastination. Assigning specific deadlines to goals drives you to act.

Setting SMART goals is an effective way to achieve your objectives.

SMART = specific, measurable, achievable, realistic, and timed.

2. Be more balanced.

———

Balance in all parts of your life is vital for overall well-being and fulfilment. Look at all the parts of your life that make you into a whole person. You are not only your professional or work-related self. You have many roles, both in and out of work.

Here's how to assess and improve work-life balance:

Health: Take care of your physical health by a balanced diet, exercising regularly, and getting enough sleep.

Relationships: Foster healthy relationships with family, friends, and significant others. Ensure you maintain personal boundaries.

Personal Growth: Allow time for self-improvement: self-care activities like reading, meditating, or attending personal growth workshops.

Leisure and Recreation: take part in hobbies, sports, and activities that bring you joy and relaxation. Spend time on what you love, try new things, and relax from everyday worries.

Finance: Gain financial balance through realistic budgets, saving, wise investments, and avoiding excessive debt. Assess your spending, prioritise expenses, and ensure financial decisions match long-term goals. Seek professional advice if needed, and practice responsible financial management.

Community: Connect with your community and contribute positively to society. Take part in volunteer work, community events, or social causes that resonate with you. Balancing personal and community involvement helps create a sense of purpose and connection.

Achieving balance does not mean equal attention or time in each area. It requires self-awareness, flexibility, and regular reassessment of priorities.

3. Do not neglect your life.

It's vital to do more than work. For example, connect to others: your partner, friends, and family. Be aware of the communities of which you are a part. These may be people in your neighbourhood, your workmates, your hobby group, or people who share your beliefs and values.

Take a step back and consider how you've been using your time. Are there certain parts of your life that you've been neglecting, perhaps unintentionally? It's crucial to recognise and address these areas to achieve a more balanced and fulfilling life.

Here are a few key points to consider:

Personal Relationships: Have you been ignoring your loved ones? Whether it's your family, friends, or romantic partner, it's important to nurture these relationships. Give quality time for important conversations and shared activities. Show them you value them by being present and actively engaged in their lives.

Self-Care: It's easy to get caught up in the chaos of life and forget to take care of yourself. Prioritise self-care activities like exercise, relaxation, and hobbies. Take the time to rest, rejuvenate, and do things that nourish your mind, body, and soul.

Health and wellness: Regular exercise, a balanced diet, and sufficient rest are essential for maintaining good health. Make time for activities that promote mental well-being, such as mindfulness, meditation, or therapy if needed. Don't neglect any health concerns. Seek professional help when required.

Pursuit of Passions: Life can get busy, and you may have put aside your dreams in favour of responsibilities. Neglecting what you are enthusiastic about can lead to a feeling of emptiness or unfulfillment. Carve out time to pursue your hobbies and desires, writing, painting, playing an instrument, or exploring new interests. Doing this will bring a sense of purpose and fulfilment back into your life.

Career and Personal Growth: Are you neglecting your professional and personal growth? Continuously learning and developing new skills are crucial in today's fast-paced world. Invest time in acquiring knowledge, expanding your network, and growing professionally. Set goals for personal development and actively work towards them.

Life is about finding a balance that works for you. Neglecting certain aspects can cause frustration and disappointment. By setting priorities and making time for neglected areas of your life, you can achieve a more fulfilling and balanced life. Start investing in yourself and the things that truly matter to you.

4. Time with your family.

Love them or hate them. They are part of you and your life. Families come together, even when separated by country or continent, to celebrate and mark life events such as births, marriages, or deaths.

Making memories and strengthening relationships requires spending quality time with your family. However, with the hustle and bustle of daily life, it's easy to neglect this. To reconnect and strengthen the bond with your loved ones, here are some suggestions on how to spend time with your family.

Establish family traditions: Create regular practices that everyone can enjoy. For example, weekly game nights, cooking together at weekends, or going for a family walk after dinner. These traditions provide a sense of stability and togetherness.

Plan family outings: Organise occasional trips or outings. These could be a visit to a nearby park, beach, or zoo. Such outings provide an opportunity for everyone to relax and enjoy each other's company outside of the usual routine.

Share a meal: Set aside time for family dinners regularly. Switch off all distractions such as the TV and mobile phones, and enjoy a meal together, engaging in meaningful conversations, to foster open communication and allow everyone to stay connected with each other's lives.

Embrace technology: Bring together distant family members with the help of technology. If you can't visit often, schedule regular video calls to maintain strong connections.

Hobbies and interests: Encourage each family member to pursue their hobbies, but also find activities everyone can enjoy together. Whether it's playing a sport, going for a hike, or attending a museum or art gallery, finding common interests enhances bonding experiences.

Volunteer together: Engaging in community service or charitable work as a family not only gives back to society but also promotes empathy within the household. Choose a cause that resonates with everyone and allocate time to work together to make a positive impact.

Have regular family meetings: Make time to discuss family matters, like planning holidays, and upcoming events, or addressing concerns. These meetings provide an opportunity for everyone to be involved and strengthen the family unit.

Unplug and connect: Set aside specific times for the family to disconnect from electronics and interact face-to-face. This could involve playing board games, doing puzzles, or simply having heart-to-heart conversations.

Spending time with family should be enjoyable and stress-free. It's not about the quantity of time spent together, but the quality of the interactions and the connections made. Prioritise this precious time and create lasting memories that will strengthen the family connection for years to come.

5. Time with friends

You are friends with those you have common interests and with whom you enjoy spending time. Keep friendships alive by making contact regularly even if you can't meet face to face.

Spending time with friends is not only enjoyable but also important for your overall well-being. It allows you to relax, unwind, and create lasting memories with the people you care about. Whether it's a planned or impromptu get-together, here are a few ideas to make the most of your time with friends.

Organise a meal: Gather your friends for a meal at a favourite restaurant or someone's home. Share stories, catch up on each other's lives, and enjoy good food together. This relaxed environment provides the perfect opportunity to bond and create deeper connections.

Plan a film night: Prepare some tasty snacks and invite your friends over. You can watch a combination of classic films, and new releases, or even binge-watch a TV series. Discussing the films afterwards can lead to interesting conversations and shared opinions.

Go on an outdoor adventure: Depending on your preferences, plan a day hike, bike ride, or picnic in a nearby park. Spending time in nature promotes physical activity and allows you to enjoy each other's company. This can be a great opportunity to bond, play games, and share laughter.

Learn something new: enrol in a cooking, painting, or dance class together. Learning a new skill or hobby with your friends will not only be educational but also create memorable experiences. It offers a chance to support and encourage each other while having fun along the way.

Volunteer or take part in community projects: Make a positive impact by volunteering together. Choose a cause that resonates with your group and helps those in need. This shared experience will strengthen your bonds as you work towards a common goal.

Have a game night: Gather your friends for a friendly competition by hosting a game night. Whether it's board games, card games, or video games, this will create a fun and relaxed atmosphere where everyone can enjoy themselves. Playful rivalry can bring out laughter and camaraderie.

Just relax and talk: Sometimes, the best way to spend time with friends is to sit down and have a genuine conversation. Having heartfelt conversations over coffee, tea, or a walk in the park can be very rewarding. Share your thoughts, dreams, and worries, and offer a listening ear to your friends.

Whatever way you choose to spend time with friends, it's important to prioritise the moments spent together. Being present, empathetic, and supportive will make your time together more meaningful and enjoyable.

6. Time with your partner

Don't let a busy life keep you from spending quality time with your partner. Make it a priority to keep your relationship alive. It's important to have time together and time apart, to do those things that interest you.

It allows for better communication, connection, and building of memories together. Here are six ways you can spend quality time with your partner:

Plan a date night: Set aside one evening each week or month to go on a special date with your partner. This could be dinner at a fancy restaurant, the cinema, or even a picnic in the park. The key is to create a dedicated time for just the two of you to focus on each other.

Take up a new hobby together: It could be cooking or gardening, or adventurous like rock climbing or learning a new language. This allows you to bond over a shared interest and create new experiences together.

Travel together: Plan a weekend getaway or a holiday. Explore fresh places and create unforgettable memories. Travelling allows you to escape from the routines of daily life and spend undivided time with your partner.

Have technology-free time: In today's digital age, it's easy to get caught up in the distractions of technology. Set aside specific times during the day or week when both of you put away your phones and other devices and focus solely on each other. This allows for uninterrupted conversation and quality time together.

Cook or bake together: Spend an evening cooking or baking a meal together. Experiment with new recipes, share kitchen duties and enjoy creating something delicious. It's a fun way to connect while sharing a common goal.

Engage in meaningful conversations: Use some time each day to have important conversations. Talk about your dreams, goals, fears, and aspirations. Listen attentively and share your thoughts as well. Engaging in deep conversations fosters emotional intimacy and strengthens your bond.

7. Interests and Hobbies

Don't forget to take care of yourself and pursue your hobbies, even if you enjoy spending time with others. Your interests and hobbies are not just ways to pass the time, they reflect your true self and what brings you joy and fulfilment. Unfortunately, it is all too easy to neglect these.

Daily life includes to-do lists, work commitments, and personal responsibilities. You find yourself multitasking and juggling many priorities, leaving little time or energy for the things that truly make you happy.

Neglecting your interests and hobbies can have serious consequences for your overall well-being. Your passions and hobbies provide you with an escape from the stresses and pressures of your everyday life. They give you a chance to disconnect and recharge, allowing you to return to your daily routine with renewed energy and enthusiasm.

Engaging in your interests and hobbies allows you to tap into your creativity and self-expression. It is through these activities that you can explore new ideas, challenge yourself, and discover hidden talents. By neglecting them, you limit your potential for growth and personal development.

Your interests and hobbies have positive effects on your mental and physical health. They bring a sense of fulfilment and happiness that can enhance your overall quality of life. Activities like playing music, painting, reading, gardening, or playing sports can bring you happiness and a sense of meaning.

Doing what you love lowers stress, boosts confidence, and enhances your thinking skills. They provide an outlet for self-care and self-expression, promoting emotional well-being and a healthy balance in your life.

Do not neglect your interests and hobbies. You must find time for these activities, alongside your other commitments. This may require setting boundaries, saying no to certain obligations, or simply attempting to make room for your passions.

Your interests and hobbies, enrich your life in countless ways. You allow yourself the freedom to explore, create, and enjoy the activities that truly make you happy. They are an essential part of who you are and deserve to be cherished and embraced.

8. Keep your sense of humour.

Find something to laugh about each day. Laughter helps you to relax and when you see the funny side of a situation, so it seems less stressful.

"Don't take life too seriously," - wise words you may forget about in the busyness of your daily life. When you get caught up in your responsibilities, stress, and problems, you may forget to enjoy the simple pleasures life offers.

Life is full of challenges, and it is easy to become overwhelmed by all those that come your way. However, when you take a step back and shift your perspective, you realise that most things don't truly matter in the grand scheme of things. Don't let those setbacks define you. They're just temporary.

Taking life too seriously robs you of joy, spontaneity, and the essence of being alive. It prevents you from fully appreciating the beauty and wonder that surrounds you. You experience, explore, and savour life. When you are too serious, you lose sight of this and turn moments of joy into periods of stress.

Find humour in the simplest of things and experience moments of pure happiness. Laughter becomes your medicine, helping to ease stress and give a fresh perspective. Focus on what matters - your well-being, relationships, and passions.

When you stop taking life seriously, you become more open to taking risks, trying new things, and stepping out of your comfort zone. You learn to be resilient and adaptable, knowing that setbacks are temporary, and you can overcome any obstacle.

Choose to live your life with a twinkle in your eyes and a smile on your face. Keep in mind that the moments when you least expect them often are the most beautiful things in life.

9. Join community activities.

———

It's vital to do more than work. You need to communicate and relate to others, your partner, friends, and family, but also be aware of the communities in which you are a part. When you have other interests, you will feel more motivated to leave work on time so you can actively take part in whatever your community is doing.

Joining community activities is a great way to get involved, meet new people, and make a positive impact. There are many activities for you to join, whether you want to volunteer, learn something new, or meet people with similar interests. Here are a few steps to consider when joining community activities:

Identify your interests: Think about your hobbies, passions, or causes you care about. Are you interested in environmental preservation, helping the homeless, or promoting arts and culture? Understanding what excites you will help you find activities that align with your interests.

Look for community organisations in your area that focus on your chosen interests. Browse their websites or social media pages to gather information on the activities they offer and how to get involved. This could include events, workshops, fundraisers, or ongoing programmes.

Attend meetings or events to learn more about their activities and meet members. Attend these gatherings to get a feel for the organisation's atmosphere and determine if it's a good fit for you.

Volunteering is one way to engage in community activities. Identify positions or projects that match your skills and availability. You might help at a local shelter, organise fundraising events, lead workshops, or tutor students. Volunteering not only allows you to contribute to a cause but also helps you connect with like-minded individuals.

Joining clubs or interest-based groups is a fantastic way to engage in community activities. Examples include book clubs, sports teams, gardening groups, art collectives, and music ensembles. These groups offer chances to engage in shared activities and make friends with people who have similar hobbies or interests.

Join classes or workshops offered by community organisations to learn new skills and connect with people who share your interests. Taking part in painting, cooking, or photography allows you to learn and connect with others.

Utilise social media such as Facebook Groups, that allow you to find local gatherings, events, or interest-based communities in your area. Joining community activities is about contributing, connecting, and enriching your own life.

PART TWO: Working efficiently

———

Working efficiently means completing tasks and achieving goals most productively and effectively as possible. It involves using time, resources, and energy wisely, minimising waste and maximising output.

Working efficiently requires good time management skills, prioritisation, focus, and organisation. It also involves finding optimal methods and strategies to complete tasks, reducing errors and rework, and continuously improving productivity and effectiveness.

Working efficiently helps to save time, reduce stress, and increase overall productivity and performance.

10.Get work done in the day.

Leave work on time and go home to relax, be with your partner and family, do what you want to do and enjoy a well-balanced life.

Start the day with a simple plan to create a to-do list to give structure to your day. Identify the most important and urgent tasks that need to be completed.

Minimise distractions: Find a quiet workspace where you can focus without interruptions. Turn off notifications on your phone or other devices that may distract you. If possible, let your colleagues know you need some uninterrupted time to complete your work.

Divide larger tasks into smaller, more manageable subtasks. This will prevent overwhelm and make it easier to focus on one specific aspect at a time.

Work for a focused period (25 minutes) followed by a brief break (5 minutes). Repeat this pattern for a few cycles, and then take a longer break (15-30 minutes). This method helps maintain focus and productivity.

Create blocks of uninterrupted time for intense work on complex tasks. During these periods, avoid checking emails or attending non-essential meetings.

Manage meetings effectively: If you have meetings during the day, ensure they are necessary and have a clear agenda. Keep them concise and stick to the scheduled time. If possible, schedule meetings back-to-back to free up larger chunks of uninterrupted work time.

Regularly take brief breaks (5-10 minutes) to rejuvenate your mind and avoid burnout. Stretch, take a walk, or do a quick mindfulness exercise to refresh and refocus.

Delegate and collaborate on projects to divide the workload. This will help you get more done within the working day while leveraging the skills and strengths of others.

Focus on one task at a time, complete it, and then move on to the next one. Multitasking can lead to reduced productivity and lower-quality work.

Reflect on the day: At the end of the working day, take some time to review your achievements and identify areas for improvement. Each person has their work style, so it's important to experiment and find the best techniques for you to work efficiently.

11. Write a to-do list.

***

People who write what they want to achieve are more likely to succeed. When you plan what to do each day, this enables you to keep focused on what you plan to do. It's easy to flit from one task to another and find you neglect things you should have done.

Your to-do list can be a vertical list or a mind map. The latter will more easily enable you to make connections between related tasks. Here is an example of a to-do list:

- Complete work project
- Pay bills.
- Grocery shopping
- Do the laundry.
- Call and schedule a doctor's appointment.
- Exercise for 30 minutes
- Clean out the cupboard and donate items!
- Reply to important emails.
- Book a holiday.
- Plan meals for the week.
- Organise paperwork and files.
- Buy a birthday gift for a friend.
- Pick up dry cleaning.
- Read for 30 minutes before bed.

12. Prioritise your tasks.

From your daily to-do list, select the tasks that are essential for the day and those that you can do later. Not all tasks are equal, so the order of your to-do list may not be the same as the order of priority.

This is essential for effective time management. Here are ways to help you order your tasks:

Assess their urgency and importance: Evaluate each task based on its urgency and importance. Urgency refers to how quickly the task needs to be completed, while importance relates to the impact and value of the task.

Categorise tasks: Divide your tasks into different categories based on their urgency and importance. You can use a numbering or colour-coding system to make it easier to identify priorities. For example:

Priority 1: Urgent and important

Priority 2: Important but not urgent

Priority 3: Urgent but not important

Priority 4: Not urgent and not important

Set deadlines: Assign realistic deadlines for each task. This will help you stay focused and organised, ensuring that you complete tasks on time.

Focus on priority 1: Start with the tasks that are both urgent and important. These require immediate attention and have a significant impact on your goals.

Tackle priority 2: Once you complete the priority 1 tasks, move on to the important but not urgent tasks. These contribute to your long-term goals, and you should not neglect them.

Address priority 3: Next, deal with tasks that are urgent but not as important. Try to complete them as efficiently as possible but ensure that they don't take precedence over priority 1 and 2.

Review priority 4: Finally, evaluate the tasks that are neither urgent nor important. These tasks may not require immediate attention but decide if they are worth keeping on your list or if you can eliminate them.

Adjust and update as needed: Throughout the day or week, evaluate your progress and adjust if necessary. New tasks may arise, and existing priorities might change.

It's essential to stay flexible and adaptable. Prioritising efficiently enables you to accomplish more and make the most of your day.

13. Do unpleasant tasks first.

Anatural tendency is to first do those things you like, leaving others until last. Try reversing this and decide each day to do at least one task you've been putting off for ages. Get it out of the way quickly, then enjoy the rest of the day doing what you enjoy. It may seem strange, but beginning your day or project with the hardest tasks can be highly helpful.

Getting the unpleasant tasks out of the way early frees up mental space and energy for the rest of your day. If you have a task hanging over your head, it can prevent you from fully focusing on other aspects of your work. Tackling it first can create a sense of relief and accomplishment, fuelling your motivation for the rest of the day.

Procrastination happens when you postpone unpleasant tasks, leading to more stress and less efficiency. The longer you put off an unpleasant task, the more it grows in your mind, becoming a daunting monster. By attacking it head-on, you eliminate the temptation to procrastinate and avoid unnecessary stress.

Completing unpleasant tasks early allows for more flexibility and adaptability. Throughout the day, unforeseen obstacles or urgent tasks may arise. Completing unpleasant tasks in advance gives you more time and flexibility for any unexpected surprises. By taking a proactive approach, you can tackle challenges logically and prevent an avoided task from casting a shadow over your entire day.

Tackling unpleasant tasks first cultivates a sense of discipline and self-control. It can be tempting to prioritise pleasurable or easier tasks, but doing so often leads to a lack of progress on the more challenging ones.

This may not be easy or enjoyable, but the benefits are worth it. Facing these tasks directly helps clear your mind, reduce stress, and boost productivity. So, the next time you encounter an unpleasant task, remember that tackling it first can set the tone for a more productive and fulfilling day.

14. Stop doing some things.

Think about your daily routine. You may be doing things because you've always done them. You can save time by letting go of unnecessary tasks.

Do you juggle multiple tasks and responsibilities, even those that are unnecessary? It's time to take a step back and evaluate your priorities. Stop doing what you don't have to do.

One of the biggest sources of stress and burnout is taking on tasks that are not essential or beneficial to your life. Don't forget, you have the choice to decide how you spend your time and energy, even if it's out of habit or social pressure.

Here are a few steps to help you stop doing what you don't have to do:

Identify your priorities: Take a moment to reflect on what truly matters to you. What are your long-term goals? What brings you joy and fulfilment? Once you understand these, you can recognise which tasks align and which do not.

Learn to say no: It's okay to refuse requests that do not serve your goals or values. If you're not interested or too busy, politely say no to invitations or commitments.

Delegate or outsource: You don't have to do everything yourself. If possible, delegate tasks to others who may have more time. Another option is to outsource tasks to make your workload easier.

Set boundaries: Establishing clear boundaries is protecting your time and ensuring that you focus on what truly matters. Learn to say no to distractions, such as excessive social media or unnecessary meetings.

Prioritise your tasks and allocate specific time for them, eliminating any non-essential activities.

Include self-care: Taking care of yourself is not a luxury, but a necessity. Make self-care a priority by setting aside time each day for activities that rejuvenate and recharge you.

Engage in activities that nourish your mind, body, and soul, like exercise, meditation, reading, or spending time with loved ones. By consciously choosing to stop doing what you don't have to do, you can reclaim your time, energy, and sanity. Remember that your time is valuable, and it deserves to be spent on things that matter. Use the power of saying no, setting clear boundaries, and prioritising self-care.

15. Stop some things.

W hen you step back and think about your daily routine, you may find you are doing some things because you've always done them. You can save time by letting go of unnecessary tasks.

Stop what doesn't have to be done. Life is filled with endless tasks and responsibilities, but not everything on our to-do lists is truly necessary. We often find ourselves caught up in a whirlwind of busyness, feeling overwhelmed and stressed. It's time to step back and do what truly matters.

Take a moment to reflect on your daily activities. Are there tasks that you constantly engage in but don't contribute to your overall well-being or personal growth? Time-wasting activities include scrolling through social media, binge-watching TV shows, and checking emails excessively. These activities can be problematic when they take up too much time and energy.

Evaluate your commitments and obligations. Are there any you took on out of guilt or pressure but don't align with your values or goals? It's essential to learn to say no to things that don't serve you. Understand that your time and energy are finite resources, and we should invest them in activities that bring value and joy to your life.

Rest and relaxation are equally important. In our fast-paced world, there's often a culture of glorifying constant productivity. It's crucial to allow yourself to rest and recharge, alongside being productive. Pushing yourself to the limit without allowing for breaks can lead to burnout and decreased effectiveness in the long run.

Self-care and personal well-being include activities that nourish your mind, body, and soul. Set aside time for activities that make you happy and fulfilled, like exercising, practising mindfulness, pursuing hobbies, or spending time with loved ones. By doing so, you'll feel more balanced to tackle the tasks that truly matter.

Attempt to focus on one task at a time. Multitasking often leads to decreased productivity and increased stress. Instead, give your full attention to the task at hand, complete it to the best of your ability, and then move on to the next. By doing so, you'll find that you accomplish more and experience a greater sense of satisfaction.

Life is too precious to be spent on what doesn't have to be done. By stopping non-essential activities and commitments, you create space for what truly matters. Embrace the concept of intentional living, and you'll lead a more balanced, fulfilling, and purposeful life.

16. Stop wasting time.

What could you do, instead of watching television or chatting on the phone? While some things may appear to waste time, remember the importance of taking breaks to nurture your body, mind, and spirit.

Your time is valuable and limited. You have goals, dreams, and aspirations, but you can't achieve any of them if you continue to waste time.

Every minute you spend aimlessly scrolling through social media or watching boring television is time lost. Before you know it, hours, days and even years have slipped away, and you have nothing to show for it. It's time to break free from the cycle of procrastination and laziness.

Take a moment to reflect on what truly matters to you. What are the things you want to accomplish in your life?

Create a plan, set goals, and act. Plan and stick to it. Focus on activities that align with your goals. Hold yourself accountable for how you spend each moment.

You cannot recover time once it's gone, as it is a precious resource. Each passing second is an opportunity to make a positive impact or to work towards your dreams.

Don't let it slip away unnoticed. When you feel the urge to waste time, ask yourself, "Is this bringing me closer to my goals?" If the answer is no, redirect your energy towards something more productive. Learn a new skill, read a book, exercise, or work on a project.

Surround yourself with like-minded individuals who inspire and motivate you. Their drive and determination will light a fire within you and push you towards success. Seek guidance from mentors who have achieved what you want to accomplish.

Stop making excuses and letting fear hold you back. Embrace failure as a learning opportunity and keep pushing forward. Remember that every successful person has faced setbacks along the way. It's how they use their time and bounce back that sets them apart.

Life is too short to waste on trivial matters. Your time is now. Start living with purpose and intention. Chase your dreams relentlessly and let nothing stand in your way.

17. Monitor activities.

By watching how you spend your day, you might realise how much time and energy you waste. This can be because of repeating tasks, doing unrelated jobs at different times, or walking back and forth to put things away. Be creative and discover more effective ways to do things.

By keeping track of your actions and progress, you can identify areas for improvement, adjust your routine, and stay on track towards your goals.

Here are a few effective methods to monitor what you're doing.

Time tracking: Use a timer or time-tracking app to record how much time you spend on specific tasks or activities throughout the day. This helps you understand where your time is being used and whether you need to allocate more or less time to certain activities.

Checklists: Create a daily, weekly, or monthly task list, detailing all the tasks you need to do. As you complete each task, mark it off the list. This not only provides a visual representation of your progress but also motivates you to complete the remaining tasks.

Journaling: Maintain a journal where you can write your daily activities, thoughts, and reflections. This helps you keep track of your mindset, emotions, and any obstacles you encounter. It also provides a foundation for self-reflection and identifying patterns in your behaviour.

Trackers: Track your progress visually with progress trackers for long-term goals. This could be a calendar where you mark off each day you've worked towards your goal or a graph showing your progress. Seeing your progress visually can be incredibly motivating.

Data analysis: In certain areas of life, like fitness or finances, tracking is crucial. Use apps or tools to measure relevant data. Keeping track of steps, calories, or savings can help you identify areas for improvement and make necessary changes.

The key is to monitor what you're doing consistently and review the information you gather regularly. This way, you can make informed decisions, identify areas for growth, and continuously improve your performance.

18. Be more efficient.

Work out more efficient ways to do things. It's too easy to carry on doing things a certain way because that's the way it's always been done.

To be more efficient, prioritise tasks, manage time effectively, and use resources efficiently. Here are some strategies to improve your efficiency:

Set clear goals: Identify your objectives and break them down into smaller, actionable tasks. Prioritise tasks based on their importance and urgency.

Plan and schedule: Create a timetable outlining your day and allocate specific time slots for each task. Stick to it as much as possible to avoid wasting time or getting overwhelmed.

Avoid multitasking: Research shows that multitasking can decrease productivity. Focus on one task at a time and give it your full attention before moving on to the next one.

Minimise distractions: Remove distractions from your workspace. Clear unnecessary tabs, silence phone alerts, and communicate your need for uninterrupted work. Letting others handle certain responsibilities can free up your time for more specialised tasks.

Use technology and tools:

Make your work easier by using tools, such as task management apps or project management software. Automate repetitive tasks.

Use the Pomodoro Technique: This time management method involves working in 25-minute intervals, followed by a quick break. This helps improve focus and prevent burnout.

Take care of yourself: Ensure you are getting enough sleep, exercise, and proper nutrition. When you are well-rested and healthy, your productivity and efficiency levels will be higher.

Continuously improve: Regularly evaluate your progress and identify areas for improvement. Seek feedback from colleagues or supervisors and try new techniques to improve efficiency.

Learn to say no: Avoid over-committing yourself by learning to say no when necessary. Understand your limits and ensure you have enough time and energy to complete your existing commitments effectively.

These strategies can help you work faster and better, reducing stress.

19. Set a time limit for each task.

Tasks expand to fill a large amount of time. If you put a bit of pressure on yourself to finish something within a limited time, or at least do as much of it as you can, it will amaze you at how much you achieve.

Setting yourself a time limit for each task can be a great way to stay focused, improve productivity, and manage your time effectively. Here are a few steps to help you set time limits for your tasks:

Identify the tasks: Start by making a list of the tasks you need to complete. Break them down into smaller, manageable chunks if necessary. Prioritise them based on urgency and importance.

Estimate time required: Take a moment to estimate how much time you think each task will take. Be realistic but also try to challenge yourself by setting slightly shorter time limits than you may initially think.

Set deadlines: Assign time limits to each task. This could be as hours or minutes allocated to each task or **by specifying the time by which you need to finish it.**

Consider your natural energy levels throughout the day. Do the more complex or demanding tasks during your peak energy hours, while leaving simpler tasks for when your energy may be lower.

Use a timer or a time management app to keep track of your allotted time for each task. Stick to your predetermined time limits and try not to get caught up in unnecessary distractions.

Review and adjust: After completing each task, take a moment to reflect on whether the time limit you set was realistic or if you need to adjust it for similar tasks in the future. This ongoing evaluation will help you refine your time management skills.

Setting time limits is about finding a balance between efficiency and task completion.

20. Take regular breaks.

Set a time to go away from your desk and do something more active for five or ten minutes every hour to wake up your brain and your body. This stops you from feeling tired and keeps different parts of your brain and body working efficiently. If your principal task is very physical, spend the break time sitting quietly, reading, or just closing your eyes and relaxing.

Taking regular breaks throughout the day is essential for maintaining overall well-being. Here are a few reasons you should take regular breaks:

Increased productivity: It may seem counterintuitive, but taking breaks can improve your output. According to research, not taking breaks during long work sessions can cause mental fatigue and reduced efficiency. By taking brief breaks every hour or so, you give your mind a chance to recharge and return to tasks with renewed energy and focus.

Improved creativity: Breaks provide an opportunity for your mind to wander and explore new ideas. Stepping away from your work for a few minutes allows your brain to make new connections and think more creatively. You may come back to your tasks with fresh insights and find innovative solutions to problems.

Better concentration: Continuous work for long hours can lead to a decline in attention span and concentration. Give yourself a chance to rest and refocus. Short breaks can help prevent mental burnout and allow you to maintain a higher level of concentration throughout the day.

Physical health benefits: Sitting or remaining in one position for extended periods can take a toll on your physical health. Regular breaks provide an opportunity to stretch, move around, and promote blood circulation. Improving your physical well-being can be as easy as going for a walk or doing household chores.

Enhanced well-being: Regular breaks help you relax, reduce stress, and prevent feeling overwhelmed. Breaks allow you to take care of your mental and emotional needs, leading to greater resilience and improved work-life balance.

Set a schedule and stick to it. Instead of mindlessly scrolling through social media or browsing the internet, use your breaks to relax and rejuvenate. Find what works best for you, whether it's meditation, listening to music, going for a quick jog, or any activity that helps you recharge.

Your mind and body will thank you, and you'll be more productive, creative, and, overall, happier in the long run.

21. Work with a deadline.

Knowing a precise date or time by which you must finish a task is highly effective in enabling you to get things done. When you are working for someone else, they will probably impose the deadline on you. However, if you work for yourself, it's much easier to procrastinate. Set your own deadline and keep reminding yourself that you must get the task completed by that date.

Working to a deadline can be challenging, but it is also a skill you can master with dedicated effort and careful planning. To effectively work towards a deadline, here are some strategies that can help you stay focused and efficient:

Understand the deadline by fully understanding the task at hand. Clarify with your superiors if necessary to ensure you have a clear vision of what needs to be accomplished by the deadline.

Break it down into smaller, more manageable sub-tasks or milestones. This will allow you to track your progress along the way.

Create a timetable for completing each task, ensuring that you allow enough time for any unexpected delays or revisions. Decide which sub-tasks are most critical.

Set realistic goals: While it's important to be ambitious, it's equally important to set realistic goals. Be mindful of your capabilities and the resources available to you. Break the work into reasonable chunks and assign an appropriate amount of time for each.

Eliminate distractions: When working towards a deadline, minimise distractions as much as possible. Find a quiet and dedicated workspace, and turn off notifications on your electronic devices, for uninterrupted work time.

Use time-management techniques like the Pomodoro Technique. Experiment with various methods to determine which one works best for you.

Delegate when possible, if you have the option, some tasks to others who can assist you. By delegating, you can save time and you accomplish all aspects of the project efficiently.

Communicate and collaborate with those involved in the project. This will help you resolve any issues that may arise along the way.

Continuously monitor your progress against the set schedule and adjust as needed. If you notice that you're falling behind, reassess your strategy, and allocate more time or resources if necessary.

Celebrate as you achieve each milestone or complete each sub-task, take a moment to acknowledge your progress. Reward yourself or your team for their hard work, as this can provide a morale boost to keep you motivated.

Working to a deadline requires discipline, focus, and effective time management. Increase your chances of meeting deadlines by using these strategies and staying positive.

22. Get help from others.

———

Unlike delegating, sometimes you need help to get going on those tasks that you've been putting off.

A common reason for procrastination is not knowing what to do. Instead of being a martyr and doing everything yourself, find someone proficient in what you are trying to do. Don't expect other people to be able to read your mind, make a request for what sort of help you want. Be prepared the answer might be no.

You don't have to face everything alone. Asking for assistance from others can not only lighten the load, but it can also provide fresh perspectives and solutions to the problems you're facing.

Here are a few steps to consider when seeking help from others:

Identify the problem: Clearly define the issue you're facing and understand why you need help. This will help you effectively communicate your needs to others.

Assess your available resources: Decide who might have the expertise or knowledge to assist you. If you're struggling, ask for help from friends, family, colleagues, or professionals.

Reach out: Once you've identified potential sources of help, ask for help. Reach out to them through phone calls, emails, social media, or in person. Be honest, concise, and specific about what you're asking for help with.

Explain why you need their help: Communicate why you've chosen to ask them for help. Explain how their skills, knowledge, or resources can contribute to solving the problem at hand. This will make them more likely to be willing and motivated to support you.

Keep in mind that the person you're seeking help from may have their commitments and priorities, so be considerate and respectful in your request.

Communicate your appreciation for their willingness to help and be open to any limitations they may have.

Be open to feedback and suggestions: Once you receive help, be receptive to feedback and new ideas. Different perspectives can expand your understanding of the problem and help you come up with creative solutions.

Seeking help is a sign of strength, not weakness. By reaching out to others, you're using the power of collective wisdom and support, which can lead to more successful outcomes.

23. Delegate more effectively

D elegating is a vital part of having more time for yourself and getting other people to do those tasks that somebody must do but not necessarily you. To delegate more effectively, you must be very clear about exactly what you want the other person to do.

Teach them how to do it, watch how they perform, and then let them get on with it. Regular checks, especially initially, are useful to make sure they are doing what you want them to do.

Here are some ways to help you delegate more effectively:

Identify the tasks to delegate: Look for those who are someone with the skills and resources that handle time-consuming routines.

Choose the right person for the task: select someone who can handle the delegated task effectively. Provide simple instructions and expectations to ensure a successful outcome.

Communicate your expectations, goals, and deadlines to the person you are delegating to. Provide all the information, resources, and instructions to ensure they understand what is required. Encourage them to ask questions and seek clarification if needed.

Provide support and resources: This could include access to documents, training, or help from other team members. Regularly check in to see if they need any additional help or guidance throughout the process.

Delegate responsibility along with tasks to inspire your team members. Trust their abilities and allow them to decide and solve problems independently. This not only increases their confidence but also frees up their time to focus on other important tasks.

Learn from the process after delegating a task and reflect on what worked well and what could improve. Adjust your approach to refine and enhance your delegation skills.

Delegation is about more than transferring tasks; it also encourages growth, development, and collaboration. By mastering delegation, you build trust and create a more efficient team.

24. Clear your desk completely.

Clearing your desk completely can be a refreshing and productive exercise. It allows you to start with a blank slate, remove distractions, and create a calm and organised workspace. Here are the steps to take:

Prepare: Gather cleaning supplies such as a dustbin, cleaning solution, and folders, trays, or storage containers.

Remove everything: Begin by removing all items from your desk. This includes papers, stationery, office supplies, gadgets, and belongings.

Sort and categorise: As you remove items, sort them into different categories, such as papers, office supplies, personal items, and miscellaneous.

Clean your desk: Once everything is off, dust it thoroughly with a cloth and use an appropriate cleaning solution to wipe away any dirt or stains.

Declutter: Go through each category of items and decide which ones you truly need. Toss any items that serve no purpose and set aside items you want to donate or recycle. Be ruthless in your decision-making to keep only what's necessary.

Organise: Now that you have decluttered, decide on a system to keep your essentials in order. Use folders or trays for documents, keep office supplies close, and assign a spot for gadgets and personal items.

Find a home for everything: Assign a place for each item on your desk and make sure it's easily accessible. This will help you develop a habit of returning items to their proper place, reducing clutter in the future.

Simplify your workspace: Keep your desk visually appealing by removing anything unnecessary. Avoid overcrowding with too many decorations or excessive supplies. A minimalist approach will create a calming environment.

Clean and maintain: Regularly clean your desk and ensure it stays clutter-free. Set aside a few minutes each day to tidy up.

Enjoy your new workspace: Sit at your cleared desk and appreciate the clean and organised environment you have created. This fresh start will boost your productivity and help you focus better on your tasks.

Maintaining a cleared desk is an ongoing process. Make it a habit to declutter and organise regularly to create an efficient and enjoyable workspace.

25. Throw away lots.

The reason for your clutter may be that you have too much 'stuff.' Be ruthless and dispose of anything out of date, such as journals, papers, old statements, clothes, and food. Recycle or compost what you can and take usable household goods and clothes to a charity shop.

If you feel overwhelmed, it's time to start sorting through the mess and donate, sell, or throw away everything you can do without.

Start with clothes, the ones you never wear. Perhaps they no longer fit, or you dislike the style or colour. They take up space but no longer bring you joy. Get rid of the shirts, trousers, and dresses, and make room for clothes you love. Then tackle your books. Some you've read, some you have read the first page and know you will never turn another. Get rid of them to others who might enjoy them.

Get rid of old gadgets and cables that you will never use again and are collecting dust.

Free up your space: Is your garage full of boxes and tools? It's time to let go of those things you no longer use or need. You keep the memories and clear the space for new projects.

As you clear out what no longer brings you joy, you may come across long-forgotten objects that remind you of other times.

Enjoy the memories and as you simplify your life, there is a space to keep those very special things. With an efficient filing system, you can find things more easily. Discover what would work best for you. A traditional filing cabinet works well so long as you can put your paperwork into files labelled by subject. You may prefer to store everything digitally.

Whether digitally or as paperwork, a filing system is essential for staying organised and maintaining efficiency both at home and at work.

Here are some tips to help you create and maintain an effective filing system:

Assess your needs: Consider what documents or materials you need to organise. Are they personal documents, work-related files, bills, or a combination of everything? Understanding your specific needs will help you determine the best approach for your filing system.

Choose a storage solution: Decide the type of filing system that suits you. Some options include filing cabinets, file boxes, binders, or digital filing systems. Consider the space available, the number of files you need to store, and your accessibility preferences. If you choose a digital filing system, ensure you have backup procedures in place.

Develop a logical structure: Create categories or folders that align with your needs. You can categorise by topic, date, purpose, or any other relevant criteria. For physical files, use labels or index tabs to clearly mark each category. In digital systems, create folders and sub-folders to organise your files logically.

Naming your files: Consistency is key when naming your files. Use clear and concise names that accurately describe the contents of each file. This will make it easier to find what you need later. Avoid using generic names like "Miscellaneous" to prevent confusion.

Prepare a filing schedule: Dedicate regular time for filing and organising your documents. This could be a weekly or monthly task, depending on your needs. Consistently addressing new documents will help prevent a backlog and maintain the efficiency of your filing system.

Regularly declutter: Periodically review your files to determine if you can discard or archive any of them. Get rid of any outdated or unnecessary documents to avoid cluttering your system. This will also ensure that your filing system remains manageable in the long run.

Backup your digital files: If you are using a digital filing system, back up your files. Use external hard drives, cloud storage, or both, depending on your preferences and requirements. This will protect your files in case of computer malfunctions or data loss.

Maintain consistency: Train yourself and others who might use the filing system to follow the established structure. Return files to their proper places after using them, so they are always accessible and organised.

A well-organised system will save you time and reduce stress when searching for important documents. It allows for easy retrieval, enhances productivity, and provides peace of mind, knowing everything has its place.

26. Keep accounts up to date.

Don't delay paying your bills. Either set up direct debit arrangements to pay recurring expenses or pay as soon as you receive the bill. Keep up to date with your accounts and credit card payments.

Keeping bills and accounts up to date is a crucial aspect of avoiding unnecessary stress. Here are some tips to help you stay on top of your expenses:

Create a system: Develop a system that works for you to keep track of your bills and accounts. Keep all financial documents together, using either a physical or online method that you prefer.

Set reminders for yourself to ensure that you never miss a payment deadline. Use calendar apps to set up alarms or notifications for bill due dates.

Review bills and statements regularly: Don't just pay your bills blindly; take the time to review them carefully. Make sure the charges are accurate, and if you notice any discrepancies, contact the company or service provider immediately to sort out the issue.

Set up automatic payments for your regular bills. This can save you time and effort, as it ensures it makes payments on time, requiring no action on your part. However, monitor your accounts regularly to ensure payments are being processed correctly.

Keep an emergency fund: Life can be unpredictable, and unexpected expenses may arise. An emergency fund will help you pay for unexpected costs without disrupting your budget or bill payments.

Track your income: Staying aware of your income is just as important as tracking expenses. Make sure you have a clear picture of the money coming in. This will provide you with better financial planning and prevent missed bill payments because of a lack of funds.

Review recurring expenses such as subscriptions, memberships, or services you no longer need or use. Cancelling these unnecessary expenses can free up funds.

Communicate with service providers: If you're struggling to pay a bill on time, don't avoid the situation. Instead, contact the service provider and discuss your situation. They may work out a payment plan or help you stay current on your bills.

27. Spend less time on the Internet.

Keep focused on your Internet searches. The internet has become a vital tool for research and information gathering. Stop yourself from going off on a tangent exploring interesting-looking sites that aren't directly connected with the task at hand.

It's easy to get lost in the world of the Internet. From social media to streaming platforms and endless web browsing, you can spend hours glued to your screen without realising it. If you want to regain control of your time and spend less time on the Internet, here are some practical tips to consider:

Set clear goals and priorities: Determine what you want to achieve in your life outside of the Internet. Write your goals and remind yourself of them regularly. Having a clear sense of purpose will help you focus on meaningful activities instead of mindlessly scrolling through the web.

Allocate specific time slots for using the Internet. Set limits on how much time you want to spend online and stick to them. For example, you could decide to only use social media for 30 minutes in the morning and 30 minutes in the evening. By setting boundaries, you'll be more mindful of your online activity.

Minimise the temptations that pull you towards the Internet. Keep your phone out of sight or use apps that limit the time you can spend on certain websites or applications. If you work on a computer, use browser extensions that block time-wasting websites during specific hours.

Find offline hobbies: Engage in activities that don't involve the Internet. Explore other interests such as reading books, practising a musical instrument, painting, or exercising. Discovering new hobbies will not only keep you occupied but also open your mind to new experiences and personal growth.

Prioritise real-life connections: Instead of relying solely on virtual interactions, try to spend quality time with friends and family in person. Meet, go for walks, have meaningful conversations, or engage in group activities. Real-life connections are essential for your well-being and can provide a refreshing break from the virtual world.

Practice mindfulness: Pay attention to your online habits and notice how they make you feel. Are you using the Internet to escape from reality or to avoid certain emotions? By being aware of your motivations, you can better control your habits and make conscious choices about your Internet usage.

Seek support: If you find it challenging to spend less time on the Internet, consider joining support groups or seeking professional help. You can get help to manage your digital habits through therapy and counselling services.

Spending time on the Internet is not inherently bad. However, when it becomes excessive and starts negatively affecting other areas of your life, it's crucial to regain control. Spend less time online and have a more balanced and fulfilling life offline with these strategies.

28. Check emails only twice a day.

Emails take so much time. Make it a routine to check new emails at certain times of the day; set up folders and rules to filter emails out of your main inbox; unsubscribe from emails that you don't have the time to read.

A time management tip is checking emails just twice a day. Research has shown that frequent email interruptions can significantly disrupt your work. By dedicating specific time slots for emails, you can regain control of your time and increase efficiency.

Here are some benefits of doing this:

Improved focus: Constantly checking emails interrupts your concentration and diverts your attention from important tasks. Set specific times to check email so you can focus on important projects without interruptions.

Reduced stress: Constant email checking not only wastes time but also increases stress. It can lead to feeling overwhelmed and constantly reactive. By limiting email checking to two dedicated periods, you regain a sense of control and reduce anxiety.

Managing your time better: Limiting email check-ins to twice daily improves organisation and efficiency in communication. This practice helps you respond to emails more efficiently. You save time and avoid unnecessary exchanges.

To implement this fresh approach efficiently, here are some guidelines:

Set specific email check-in times: Select time slots during the day to dedicate solely to managing emails. Ensure these times do not coincide with your most productive periods, instead allowing for focused work before and after.

Communicate your new email routine: Inform your colleagues and external contacts about your new email strategy. Clearly communicate your response times to manage expectations and reduce the need for immediate replies.

Establish a routine for processing emails during designated check-in times. Sort emails into folders or categories, prioritise them according to urgency and respond to the most critical ones promptly. Delegate or schedule less urgent emails for later if needed.

By adopting this practice, you will improve your productivity, regain focus, and reduce unnecessary stress. While it may take some change initially, the long-term benefits are worthwhile.

When you are behind with your paperwork, spend half an hour each day dealing with it, besides the new stuff that goes into a different pile, and you deal with it daily. Dealing with paperwork can feel like a daunting and never-ending task. However, by dealing with a manageable amount each day, you can stay organised.

Here's a plan to help you tackle your paperwork more efficiently:

Set a specific time and place: Dedicate a specific time slot each day to focus solely on paperwork. Choose a quiet and comfortable space where you can work without distractions.

Prioritise your tasks: Start by creating a to-do list or identifying the most urgent paperwork that needs to be addressed. This could include bills, contracts, invoices, or any other documents that require your attention.

Gather the tools: Equip yourself with all the tools to complete the paperwork efficiently. This may include a filing system, a pen, a calculator, sticky notes, and any other supplies you might need.

Sort and organise your paperwork into different categories or folders. This could be based on document type, due date, or priority level. Use sticky notes or labels to mark important sections or pages.

Tackle one task at a time: Focus on completing one task or document at a time to avoid feeling overwhelmed. Give each task your undivided attention until you complete it or until you have reached a logical stopping point.

Take breaks: Break up your paperwork sessions with brief breaks to rest your mind and prevent burnout. During these breaks, stretch, hydrate, or engage in a brief activity that relaxes you.

File and store: Once you have completed a task or processed a document, ensure that you file it away in a designated place. Maintain an organised filing system for easy retrieval and reference in the future.

Review and assess: At the end of each paperwork session, take a few minutes to review what you have accomplished. Assess whether there are any outstanding tasks or if any follow-up actions are required.

Maintain consistency: Commit to repeating this daily paperwork routine to prevent a backlog from building up. Consistency is key to staying on top of your paperwork and preventing it from becoming overwhelming.

Use systems or software to automate certain tasks, such as bill payments or document organisation. This can save time and reduce the amount of physical paperwork you must deal with.

Dealing with paperwork is a continuous process. Create an efficient and stress-free environment by organising your paperwork, setting priorities, and sticking to a routine.

Part 3: Decision Making

Decision-making refers to identifying and selecting the best course of action or solution from various alternatives to achieve a particular goal or objective.

It involves evaluating different options based on their advantages, disadvantages, and potential outcomes, and then making a judgment or choice based on logic, reasoning, and available information.

Effective decision-making often requires critical thinking, problem-solving skills, analysis of data, consideration of different perspectives, and the ability to weigh risks and benefits.

29. Gain Clarity.

Understand **your choices**: It's not always a simple A or B situation; there may be a middle ground option C that offers unexpected benefits.

Decision-making can feel overwhelming, especially when faced with complex choices or uncertain outcomes. It's natural to want clarity before making important decisions, as this can help reduce anxiety and ensure a more informed choice. Here are some strategies to help you be clear about your decisions:

Define your goals: Start by describing what you hope to achieve through this decision. Having a clear understanding of your goals will help you to ignore options that are not part of your objectives.

Gather information: Do thorough research and gather as much relevant information as possible about the choices you have. This may include case studies, expert consultations, seeking advice, or conducting experiments or surveys. The more information you have, the better equipped you will be to make an informed choice.

Weigh the pros and cons: Create a list of the advantages and disadvantages associated with each option. This will allow you to assess the potential benefits and drawbacks of each choice. Assigning importance to each factor can help you decide the options that link most closely with your goals.

Consider the long-term impact: Besides short-term benefits or immediate considerations, think about the long-term consequences of your decision. Consider how each option may affect your future goals, relationships, or overall well-being.

Trust your intuition: Gathering information and considering factors is important, but don't forget the power of your gut feeling. Sometimes, your intuition provides valuable insights that you may not have considered. Trust your intuition about a choice, but also consider other options.

Seek feedback from others: Consult people you trust and value their opinions. They may offer new perspectives, highlight potential blind spots, or provide support in validating your own thoughts. The final decision is yours, and it's important to sift through feedback to determine what resonates with you.

Test your options: In some cases, you may test different options on a smaller scale before making a final decision. This might involve piloting a project, trying out a new routine, or conducting an experiment. Testing reduces uncertainty and improves clarity about each option's feasibility and effectiveness.

Set a deadline: While clarity may come naturally with time, setting a deadline can help you avoid analysis paralysis. Even if you haven't achieved complete clarity, you may need to decide. Setting a deadline encourages active decision-making and helps you move forward.

Achieving complete clarity is not always possible. Life is filled with uncertainty, and no decision is entirely risk-free. These strategies can help you make decisions that align with your goals and values.

30. Group your choices together.

———

Start by grouping your choices as broad solutions rather than very specific, at this stage. When you decide the category of your desired choice, you will then be better able to narrow your choice more easily.

Grouping your choices when faced with multiple choices, can sometimes be helpful. This allows you to analyse and compare options within each group, making it easier to decide. Here are a few effective ways to group your choices.

Grouping choices into categories can help evaluate each category separately. Take, for example, deciding on a holiday destination. You can categorise options like beach destinations, historical sites, or adventure travel.

By priority level: This can make decision-making more manageable. Group options based on their high-priority, low-priority, or medium-priority status. This way, you can focus on comparing and selecting the most crucial choices first before moving on to less urgent ones.

By pros and cons: Consider creating two groups based on the advantages and disadvantages of each choice. By grouping the pros and cons, you can better compare the benefits and drawbacks of each option.

Grouping choices based on practicality makes it easier to evaluate their feasibility. This can help you eliminate choices that may not be realistic or achievable, the decision-making process more streamlined.

By personal preferences: It's helpful to group choices based on personal preferences if you favour certain criteria or characteristics. You can create groups based on what aligns most with your values, interests, or desires, allowing you to choose options that resonate with you on a personal level.

The way you group your choices will depend on the specific situation and context. Experiment with different grouping methods and use the one that best suits your decision-making process. Grouping your choices together helps you decide in a systematic and organised way, so you can choose the best option.

31. Chunk down your choice.

After you've made the key decision, narrow down your options and plan the details of what you want to do. When you do that, you can ask yourself what it is you need to find out or learn about each choice before making the final decision.

Define the problem: Start by defining the issue that needs to be addressed. Break it down into specific aspects or components to better understand the problem.

Gather information: Conduct research, talk to experts, and gather relevant data to gather as much information as possible about the situation. This will help you make an informed decision.

Identify viable options: brainstorm and generate a list of solutions or courses of action. Be imaginative and think outside conventional boundaries. Consider the pros and cons of each option.

Evaluate options: Assess each option based on various criteria, such as achievability, cost, time, and impact. Consider potential risks and benefits associated with each choice. Use analytical tools or decision-making frameworks to organise your thoughts and compare options.

Choose the best option: After evaluating all the options, select the one that aligns most closely with your goals, values, and objectives. Consider the potential consequences of your choice and whether they are acceptable.

Implement the decision: Take the steps to put your choice into action. Develop a detailed plan, allocate resources, and communicate the decision to the stakeholders involved. Monitor and adjust the implementation process as needed.

Evaluate the outcome: Assess the results and outcomes of your decision. Determine whether it achieved the desired result or if any adjustments or modifications are required. Learning from your decision-making process can help improve future choices.

Decision-making is an on-going process, and it may be necessary to revisit and revise certain steps along the way.

32. Make a list of pros and cons.

Making a list of the good and bad things of each choice is a common way to decide, and it means that you will make an informed choice. Not everyone agrees on this. Some seek opinions from others who have been through something similar, while others rely on their intuition. Most of us use a bit of each of these.

Pros:

- Provide a clear overview of the advantages and disadvantages.
- Facilitate the decision-making process.
- Helps to identify the strengths and weaknesses of a particular subject.
- Encourages critical thinking and analysis.
- Enables effective evaluation and comparison of options.

- Organises thoughts and ideas in a structured manner.
- Allows for efficient communication of complex information.
- Helps to weigh the potential benefits against the potential risks.
- Helps identify potential opportunities and threats.
- Promotes a balanced and informed approach to decision-making.

Cons:

- Can be time-consuming to create an extensive and detailed list.
- This may lead to bias if not objectively compiled.
- Can oversimplify complex issues or factors.

- May not account for subjective preferences or individual circumstances.
- Can depend on accurate and up-to-date information.
- Might overlook or underestimate some pros or cons.
- This can lead to analysis paralysis if they place too much emphasis on the list-making process.
- Potential for overlooking more nuanced or intangible factors.
- Prone to personal interpretation and bias in selecting and ranking pros and cons.
- May not capture all potential pros and cons, especially in complex or multifaceted situations.

33. Notice your internal voice.

Take a moment to listen to the voice that narrates your thoughts, doubts, desires and talks inside your head. Recognise and become familiar with that internal voice. It can affect your outlook, emotions, and actions. Sometimes this internal voice can be supportive and encouraging, building you up and reminding you of your strengths. Other times, it can be critical and discouraging, planting seeds of doubt and self-judgment.

Noticing your internal voice, allows you to gain valuable insight into how you perceive yourself and the world around you. You can identify if your internal voice is more positive or negative, encouraging or discouraging. This awareness can be the first step towards nurturing a more positive and compassionate mindset.

Your internal voice allows you to evaluate the accuracy of the thoughts it generates. Are these thoughts rational? Or are they distorted by limiting beliefs or negative assumptions? You can begin to challenge and reframe unhelpful thoughts, leading to a more positive and empowering mindset.

Another benefit of noticing your internal voice is that it can create space for self-reflection and introspection. When you listen closely to your internal voice, you can discover hidden beliefs, fears, and desires that influence your thinking and actions. This self-awareness can provide valuable insights into personal growth and development.

Notice your internal voice. What is it saying? Is it kind and supportive? Or is it critical and judgmental? By cultivating a conscious awareness of your internal voice, you can harness its power and transform it into a positive force in your life.

Trust your instincts when deciding, as they are just as important as what others say or what you want to do. Each of these is a way in which people decide.

Trust your instincts when deciding, as they are just as important as what others say or what you want to do. Each of these is a way in which people decide.

34. Notice Your Gut Feelings

Your gut feeling is an instinctive response that you should not ignore. It is the subtle, intuitive sensation you experience deep within that guides you in decisions and judgments.

Trusting your instincts can guide you in different situations, like career choices and relationships.

Here are a few reasons you should start noticing your gut feelings:

Intuition: Your gut feeling is often a result of intuition, which is shaped by your experiences and subconscious processing of information. It can provide valuable insights that your logical mind might overlook. Trusting your intuition can lead to better decision-making and help you avoid unnecessary risks.

Warning Signs: Sometimes, your gut feeling acts as a warning sign when something doesn't feel right. It might create a sense of unease or discomfort in situations where you need to be cautious. It's crucial to acknowledge and investigate these feelings rather than dismissing them. They could signal potential dangers or red flags.

Authenticity: Your gut feeling can be a guide to help you determine whether a person or situation feels authentic and genuine. It is often a subconscious evaluation of non-verbal cues, energy, and vibrations. Trusting your gut can help you build authentic relationships and connections.

Self-Awareness: Taking the time to notice and examine your gut feelings can increase your self-awareness. It helps you understand your emotions, desires, and needs at a deeper level. Recognising the triggers that evoke certain gut feelings can give you valuable insights into your own personality and values.

Decision-making: Gut feelings can serve as an additional data point alongside rational analysis when deciding. By combining logic and intuition, you can make better choices.

Personal Growth: Being attuned to your gut feelings can enhance your personal growth journey. It allows you to explore your innermost desires, passions, and aspirations, enabling you to align your actions with your truest self.

Create calm: Find moments of quiet reflection to tune in to your inner voice. Meditation, journaling, or going for a walk outside in nature can help create the mental space necessary to notice your gut feelings.

Tune in to your bodily sensations, emotions, and mental responses when deciding. Notice any subtle shifts or changes.

Review your decisions and outcomes in the past and reflect on how your gut feelings played a role. This analysis can help you distinguish between your instincts and outside influences.

Trust and act: Once you recognise and trust your gut feelings, then act. Even if the outcomes aren't always perfect, remember that taking a step based on your intuition is a valuable learning experience.

Noticing your gut feelings is a skill that improves with practice. Over time, you will become more attuned to your intuition and navigate life's experiences with greater clarity and confidence. Trust yourself and listen to that quiet voice within – it often knows more than you realise.

35. Consider alternatives.

Prepare a **Plan B** if your primary choice goes completely wrong so that you have an alternative to fall back on. Although you can't be sure that the choice you make will turn out to be the best choice for you. It is reassuring to know that if your first choice fails, you can fall back on another choice.

When making plans, consider alternative options. It ensures you explore different viewpoints and options, making your plan more versatile. Here are a few reasons why considering alternatives is important:

Exploring alternatives helps you discover potential risks and uncertainties tied to your plan. This allows you to develop backup strategies or contingency plans to address these risks effectively.

Improved Decision-Making: Considering alternatives helps you to evaluate different approaches and solutions. It allows you to weigh the pros and cons of each option, enabling you to make more informed decisions based on a broader understanding of the situation.

Having alternative options in mind makes your plan more flexible and adaptable to changing circumstances. Unexpected things can happen, so having backup plans helps you adapt and achieve your goals.

Exploring alternative options encourages innovative thinking. It creates fresh opportunities and prompts thinking beyond conventional limits, resulting in inventive problem-solving.

Considering alternative plans allows you to evaluate the most effective approach. By comparing options, you can find the best solution that saves resources, time, and effort while reducing risks and challenges.

Keep an open mind and be willing to consider alternatives. Trying out different options can make your original plan even better, suggesting no flaws. So, take the time to brainstorm and evaluate distinct possibilities before finalising your plan.

36. Prepare for all eventualities.

Assuming you have finally made a choice, which you can refer to as Plan A, then be as prepared for all eventualities as you can. Prepare more detail for your plan A: is there anything you need to find out before you can be sure it's right for you?

Preparing for all eventualities can be an overwhelming task, but it is crucial to have a plan in place to navigate through unexpected situations. Here are some steps to help you prepare for all eventualities:

Start by identifying different risks and potential problems in your specific situation. Consider both common and uncommon risks and prioritise them based on their likelihood and impact.

Develop a contingency plan: Once you have identified the risks, create a contingency plan for each potential eventuality. This plan should outline the steps you will take if a specific event occurs. For example, if there is a power outage, you may need to have a backup generator or a plan to move temporarily.

Gather necessary resources: Depending on the potential risks, gather the resources you may need. This could include emergency supplies like food, water, medical kits, and communication devices.

It may also involve finding emergency services, insurance providers, or friends and family for support.

Create an emergency fund: Financial preparedness is essential for unforeseen events. Establish an emergency fund that can cover unexpected expenses, such as medical bills or repairs. Aim to save at least three to six months' worth of living expenses, so you have a safety net in case of job loss or emergencies.

Keep yourself updated on current events, weather forecasts, and potential risks specific to your region.

Sign up for emergency alerts and follow reputable news sources. Stay connected with your local community to know about any significant developments that may affect you.

Create a communication plan to stay connected with your loved ones during emergencies. Pick a meeting place, create backup communication methods, and share contact info with loved ones.

Review and practice your emergency plans to ensure everyone involved knows what to do in case of an eventuality. Running drills will help familiarise you with the plan and highlight any areas that may need improvement or change.

Stay adaptable: Keep in mind that unexpected events may not always fit neatly into your prepared contingency plans. Maintaining flexibility and adaptability is vital. Regularly reassess your plans and adjust them as necessary based on new information or experiences.

Preparing for all eventualities does not mean you can predict everything that may happen. It ensures that you have a solid foundation to respond effectively when unforeseen situations arise.

Part Four: Self-help

———

Self-help refers to resources, techniques, activities, or practices aimed at promoting personal growth, self-improvement, and wellness.

It involves individuals taking active steps, often independently, to address their emotional, psychological, or behavioural issues and work towards achieving their goals and aspirations.

Self-help may encompass various areas of life, including mental health, relationships, career, spirituality, physical well-being, and overall personal development.

It typically involves engaging in activities such as reading self-help books, attending workshops or seminars, seeking counselling or therapy, practising self-reflection and introspection, setting personal goals, and adopting healthy habits and coping mechanisms.

The ultimate objective of self-help is to empower individuals to become more self-aware, confident, and resilient, leading to a happier and more fulfilling life.

37. Connect with your breath.

Breathing slowly in and out, while you count slowly to five, is a way not only to relax but also to connect with your breath and a way to manage your stress levels. Breathe out stress and breathe in peace and relaxation.

Take a moment to pause and connect with your breath. Find a comfortable position, sitting or lying down, and close your eyes if that feels comfortable. Allow your body to relax, releasing any tension or stress.

Bring your attention to your breath. Notice the sensation of the air entering your nostrils as you inhale, and the feeling of the air leaving your nostrils as you exhale. Pay attention to the rise and fall of your chest or belly with each breath.

Bring your full awareness to your breath. Notice its rhythm and depth. Is it shallow or deep? Fast or slow? Just observe without judgement.

You may notice that your mind wanders. Thoughts, worries, and distractions may come up. That's okay. Whenever you notice your mind has wandered, gently guide your focus back to your breath. Use your breath as an anchor to bring you back to the present moment.

Immerse yourself in the experience of breathing fully. Feel the soothing sensation as the breath enters and leaves your body. Feel the nourishment and life force that your breath brings with each inhale. Experience the release and letting go with each exhale.

Stay with your breath for a few more moments, being fully present and engaged with this simple act of breathing. Notice how your body and mind respond to this connection with your breath.

When you are ready, gently open your eyes and take a few moments to reorient yourself to your surroundings. Carry this sense of connection with your breath into your day, using it as a tool to bring you back to the present moment whenever you need it.

38. Reduce caffeine.

Drinking caffeinated drinks gives you the impression of having more energy, but in fact, this is a temporary energy boost. Caffeine makes your heart beat faster and can stop you from sleeping at night.

Caffeine can be a hard habit to break, but cutting down on your intake can have many health benefits. Here are a few steps to help you reduce your caffeine consumption:

Set a limit: Determine the maximum amount of caffeine you want to consume in a day. This could be a specific number of cups or a certain milligram threshold.

Slowly reduce the amount of caffeine you consume. For example, if you usually have four cups of coffee a day, cut down to three a day, for a week, then two for the following week, and so on.

Replace some caffeinated drinks with decaf or herbal options once you've reached your limit. This way, you can still enjoy the ritual of drinking a warm beverage without the stimulating effects of caffeine.

Caffeine may be hidden in energy drinks, soda, and chocolate. It can also be present in certain medications, and some flavoured waters. Read ingredient labels and be aware of these hidden sources to better manage your caffeine intake.

Include healthier habits for an energy boost, instead of relying on caffeine, This may include exercising regularly, getting enough sleep, and maintaining a balanced diet. These alternatives will provide sustainable energy with no caffeine.

Stay hydrated: Drinking enough water can help you feel more awake and alert, reducing your reliance on caffeine for a quick pick-me-up. Keep a water bottle nearby and sip on it throughout the day to ensure proper hydration.

Get help from friends, family, or a healthcare professional. They can provide guidance, encouragement, and accountability to help you stay on track.

Cutting down on caffeine may take time to adjust. Be patient with yourself and celebrate minor victories along the way. Your body will thank you for the reduced caffeine intake and you'll ultimately enjoy improved energy levels and better sleep patterns.

39. Learn to relax.

Relax by sitting comfortably and closing your eyes. Concentrate on each part of your body starting with your feet up to your head, as you consciously tense that part and then let it go as you relax.

Learning to relax is a valuable skill that can improve both your mental and physical well-being. It's important to take the time to unwind and recharge. If you find it difficult to relax, here are some tips to help you learn how to relax:

Create a calm environment: Find a peaceful space in your home where you can comfortably relax. Clear any clutter and create a relaxing ambience with soft lighting, calming scents, and comfortable seating.

Practice deep breathing: Deep breathing is a simple and effective relaxation technique. Sit or lie down in a comfortable position and take slow, deep breaths. Inhale through your nose, fill your belly with air and exhale through your mouth, releasing any tension or stress. Focus on your breath and let go of any other thoughts.

Engage in a hobby: Find a hobby or activity that you enjoy and that helps you relax. It could be painting, gardening, playing a musical instrument, reading, or cooking. Engaging in activities that you love can shift your focus away from stress and help you enter a state of relaxation.

Practice mindfulness or meditation: These are great techniques to train your mind to relax and be present in the moment. Find a comfortable position, close your eyes, and focus on your breath, or repeat a mantra. Allow your thoughts to come and go without judgment. With regular practice, you will feel more grounded and relaxed.

Exercise regularly: Physical activity is a wonderful way to reduce stress and relax the body. Find an exercise routine that suits your interests and schedule. Doing activities like yoga, running, swimming, or dancing can help release endorphins and improve your mood.

Prioritise self-care in your life. Take time each day to do something nurturing for yourself, whether it's taking a relaxing bath, reading a book, or indulging in a hobby. Set quality time for yourself regularly.

Practice time management: Stress can often result from feeling overwhelmed or having too much on your plate. Learning to manage your time effectively can help reduce stress and create more relaxation in your life. Prioritise tasks, delegate when possible, and create a schedule that allows for breaks and downtime.

Disconnecting from technology: Constant connectivity can contribute to stress and make it difficult to relax. Take breaks from screens and disconnect from technology for a set period each day. Use this time to engage in activities that promote relaxation and self-care.

Learning to relax is a process, and it may take time to find what works best for you. Be patient with yourself and make self-care a priority. With practice and consistency, you will develop the ability to relax and find more peace and balance in your life.

40. Get more sleep.

Go to bed earlier so you have enough sleep and start each new day refreshed. Avoid computer screens before you go to bed or drinking caffeine-containing drinks such as tea or coffee.

Sleep is an essential part of life, and getting enough of it is crucial for our overall health and well-being. However, in our fast-paced and demanding lives, it can sometimes be challenging to prioritise sleep. If you struggle to get enough rest, here are some tips to help you get more sleep:

Establish a consistent sleep schedule: Try to go to bed and wake up at the same time every day, even on weekends. This helps to regulate your body's internal clock and improve the quality of your sleep.

Create a bedtime routine: Develop a relaxing routine before bed to signal to your body that it's time to sleep. You can include activities like reading, taking a bath, or practising relaxation techniques.

Make your bedroom a sleep-friendly environment: Ensure that your bedroom is quiet, dark, and cool. Invest in high-quality bedding and a comfortable mattress that supports your sleeping posture. Remove any distractions, such as electronic devices, that may interfere with your sleep.

Limit exposure to blue light: Electronic devices emit blue light, which can disrupt your sleep cycle. Avoid using smartphones, tablets, or laptops before bed. Consider using blue light filters or wearing blue light-blocking glasses.

Avoid stimulants close to bedtime: Limit the consumption of caffeine, nicotine, and alcohol, as they can interfere with your ability to fall asleep and stay asleep. It's best to avoid consuming these substances at least a few hours before bedtime.

Exercise regularly: Engaging in regular physical activity during the day can promote better sleep at night. However, avoid exercising too close to bedtime, as this can make it harder to fall asleep.

Manage stress and worries: If your thoughts preoccupy you, it's difficult to fall asleep. Manage stress by journaling practising mindfulness or talking to a trusted friend or therapist.

Avoid napping close to bedtime: While brief daytime naps can be beneficial, taking long naps or napping too close to your bedtime can disrupt your sleep pattern. If you need to nap, aim for a quick power nap earlier in the day.

Evaluate your sleep environment: If you have trouble sleeping, think about any problems in your sleep environment, like uncomfortable bedding, noise, or a snoring partner. Address these issues to improve your sleep quality.

Seek professional help if needed: If your sleep problems persist, consult a healthcare professional or a sleep specialist who can assess and provide guidance.

Sleep is not a luxury, but a necessity. Prioritising your sleep will not only improve your cognitive function and overall health but also enhance your quality of life. Attempt to incorporate good sleep habits into your daily routine and enjoy the benefits of a well-rested mind and body.

41. Take more aerobic exercise.

———

Keep your heart fit and your muscles working efficiently. Exercising regularly releases endorphins, making you feel relaxed. It also keeps your body fit and maintains a healthy weight.

Aerobic exercise is a great way to improve both your physical and mental well-being. Aerobic exercises include activities such as running, swimming, cycling, dancing, and brisk walking. These exercises increase your heart rate and breathing, resulting in improved cardiovascular health.

Regular aerobic exercise has numerous benefits for your body. It helps to increase stamina and endurance, making everyday tasks easier. It also leads to a stronger heart, lower blood pressure, and improved lung function. Engaging in aerobic exercise can aid in weight management by burning calories and reducing body fat.

Aerobic exercise is not only great for your physical health but also for your mental well-being. When you work out, your brain releases chemicals that boost your mood and reduce stress. Someone has even linked regular aerobic exercise to reducing symptoms of anxiety and depression.

Include more aerobic exercise into your routine, by setting achievable goals. For example, you can aim to exercise for at least 30 minutes, five days a week. You can divide this time into smaller intervals, such as three 10-minute sessions throughout the day.

Find activities you enjoy and that fit into your schedule. Variety is key, so mix up your workouts to keep things interesting.

Consider joining a fitness class or group to stay motivated and accountable. Exercise with a friend or family member to make it more enjoyable. Designate specific times for exercise in your schedule, treating them as unchangeable appointments.

Warm up before starting any aerobic exercise and cool down afterwards to prevent injury. Start slowly if you are new to exercise increasing the intensity and duration.

Taking more aerobic exercise is an investment in your overall health and well-being. It is a practice that can benefit your body, mind, and spirit. Start today and reap the rewards of a healthier, happier life.

42. Practice Yoga.

Keep your body and mind flexible. Concentrating on yoga postures leads to a lowering of blood pressure and has a calming effect, so is an ideal pursuit for stress management.

Yoga has become a popular form of exercise for people of all ages and fitness levels. By combining postures, breathing, and meditation, it promotes strength, flexibility, balance, and overall well-being. If you're new to yoga or looking to deepen your practice, here are some tips to help you get started:

Find a suitable space: Look for a quiet and clutter-free area in your home or attend a yoga class at a studio. Make sure you have enough space to move around comfortably.

Get the right equipment: You only need a few basic items to practise yoga. Invest in a good yoga mat, comfortable clothing that allows for a full range of motion, and props like blocks and straps to support your practice.

Start with gentle poses: Begin with gentle poses like child's pose, cat-cow, and downward-facing dog to warm up your body and get into the flow of movement. Pay attention to proper alignment and listen to your body, avoiding any pain or discomfort.

Focus on your breath: Yoga is not just about physical movements; it's also about connecting breath with movement. Practice deep, slow breathing throughout your practice, inhaling and exhaling through your nose. This will help calm your mind and create a sense of relaxation.

Take it slowly: Yoga is not a competition or a race. Take your time with each pose, allowing your body to sink into the stretch. It's okay to change positions to suit your flexibility and strength. Remember, it's about the journey, not the destination.

Stay present: Yoga is a practice of mindfulness, so try to stay fully present in each moment. Let go of any distractions or thoughts about the past or future. Instead, focus on the sensations in your body, the rhythm of your breath, and the feeling of relaxation.

Include meditation: After your physical practice, take a few minutes to sit in a comfortable position and meditate. Close your eyes, bring your attention to your breath, and try to quiet your mind. This will help you cultivate a sense of inner peace and clarity.

Stay consistent: Consistency is key to yoga. Aim to practise regularly, even if it's just for a few minutes each day. The more you practise, the more benefits you will experience in terms of improved strength, flexibility, and mental well-being.

Be patient with yourself, embrace your progress, and enjoy the process of self-discovery and self-care that yoga brings.

43. Get support.

Find someone to talk to about your stress. Talking to someone who will listen and not judge you, is very beneficial to help you cope with stress and discover ways to deal with it. This could be a counsellor, therapist, coach, friend, or family member.

Support services are completely confidential, so you can feel safe discussing any concern or problem with them.

Everyone's circumstances are unique, and so are their needs for support. That's why help is related to your specific situation. No matter what you're going through, we will work with you to find the most suitable solutions and resources available.

Seeking support is a sign of strength. It takes courage to ask for help and take steps towards improving your well-being. You don't have to face your challenges alone.

If you're feeling stressed and overwhelmed, it's important to remember that you don't have to go through it alone. There are various sources of support available to help you navigate through stressful situations. Here are some suggestions on how to get stress support:

Talk to someone you trust: Reach out to a friend, family member, or someone you feel comfortable with to share what you're going through. Simply talking about your feelings and concerns can often provide relief and a fresh perspective on the situation.

Seek professional help: If your stress level becomes unmanageable and affects your daily life, consider seeking the assistance of a mental health professional. Therapists, psychologists, and counsellors are trained to help individuals cope with stress and develop strategies to overcome it.

Join a support group: Participating in a support group can provide you with the opportunity to connect with others who are facing similar challenges. Sharing experiences, thoughts, and coping strategies in a supportive environment can be immensely beneficial and help alleviate stress.

Utilise helplines: In times of immediate stress or crisis, helplines can provide instant support. Many organisations offer hotlines specifically dedicated to stress, anxiety, and mental health. Make a note of helpline numbers and use them whenever you need someone to talk to.

Take advantage of workplace resources: Many employers offer employee assistance programs that provide counselling services or referrals to therapists or support groups. Check with your human resources department to see if your workplace offers such resources.

Engaging in stress-reducing activities in your routine can provide ongoing support. Activities such as exercising, meditation, deep breathing exercises, journaling, or engaging in hobbies you enjoy can help you relax and manage stress more effectively.

Taking the time to care for your mental and emotional well-being is essential for maintaining overall health.

44. Share household chores.

When you are very busy and stressed, let go of 'being perfect.' If domestic chores take a lot of your time, then either don't do them, delegate to other members of the household, or pay for some help.

Sharing chores can lead to a more balanced and harmonious living environment. Here are a few tips on how to share household chores:

Communication is key: Sit down with your family or flatmates and have an open and honest conversation about household chores. Discuss everyone's expectations and preferences and come up with a plan that works for all.

Designate specific jobs to each person and create a calendar. This way, everyone knows what needs to be done and when. You can rotate tasks on a weekly or monthly basis to ensure fairness.

Divide and conquer: Assign jobs based on each person's skills and preferences. Some people might enjoy cooking, while others might prefer cleaning the bathrooms. Play to everyone's strengths and interests to make chores more manageable and enjoyable.

Set realistic expectations: Be clear about the standards you expect for cleanliness, frequency of completion, and any specific instructions. This helps avoid misunderstandings and ensures everyone agrees.

Encourage teamwork: Help each other out and work together. This not only speeds up the process but also fosters a sense of cooperation within the household.

Have regular check-ins to discuss any concerns or issues that may arise. This allows everyone to voice their opinions, make suggestions, and address any problems.

Show appreciation: acknowledge and appreciate each other's efforts. A simple "thank you" or a small token of appreciation can go a long way in morale and motivation.

Sharing household chores is not just about distributing the workload; it's about fostering a sense of responsibility, teamwork, and respect within the household. By working together, you can create a more organised and enjoyable living environment for everyone involved.

45. Allow extra time for travel.

A void the increased stress of being late for an appointment. Double the time you think it will take to get from A to B and arrive calm with time to spare.

To ensure a stress-free and on-time journey, it is always advisable to allow extra time for your travels. Adding extra time to your commute, road trip, or flight can improve your overall experience. Here's why it's crucial and how you can effectively incorporate this practice into your daily routine.

Unforeseen delays can occur during your journey. Traffic jams, road closures, accidents, or even bad weather can all disrupt your plans and add significant time to your trip. By allowing extra time, you give yourself the flexibility to adapt to these circumstances without feeling rushed or stressed.

Safety first: Rushing from one place to another can compromise your safety and the safety of others. When you are in a hurry, it may tempt you to speed, take shortcuts, or overlook essential safety precautions. Giving yourself more time allows for safer driving and decision-making.

Avoid unnecessary stress: We all have experienced the anxiety that comes with running late. It can affect your mood and overall well-being. By giving yourself extra time, you can eliminate unnecessary stress and enjoy a more relaxed journey. You'll have enough time to gather your belongings, double-check your route, and mentally prepare for the day ahead.

Discover unforeseen opportunities: Occasionally, allowing extra time for your journey can present unexpected opportunities. You might find a new café, explore a new scenic route, or take a relaxing walk before your appointment. Embracing these moments can add a sense of adventure and make your journey more memorable.

To make the most of this practice, here are a few practical tips:

Plan your journey: Map out your route, check for any potential delays, and estimate the time needed for each leg of your trip. This will give you a realistic idea of how much extra time you should allocate.

Anticipate peak traffic hours: If you are commuting during rush hour, it is essential to factor in additional time for potential congestion. Research and understand when traffic is typically heaviest in your area.

Be prepared: Make sure you have everything you need for the journey, such as enough fuel, snacks, water, or any necessary documentation. Being prepared in advance will save you time and potential stress.

Use technology to stay informed about delays or alternate routes by using navigation apps or public transportation apps.

Giving yourself more time for your trips can improve your travel experiences. It provides you with more control, reduces stress, and allows you to embrace any unexpected opportunities along the way. So, next time you're planning a trip, remember to give yourself a little extra time and embark on a smoother, more enjoyable journey.

46. Be more creative.

Get involved in creative hobbies because creativity is a wonderful way to let go of stress. Being creative allows you to let go of day-to-day worries for a while as you engage in whatever creative activity you enjoy.

Be more than just a passive observer of the world around you; let your imagination run wild and unleash your creative spirit. Here are a few tips to help you be more creative:

Embrace curiosity: Cultivate a sense of wonder and allow yourself to ask questions. Be curious about your surroundings and let your mind wander. Explore new interests and indulge in hobbies that attract your curiosity.

Step out of your comfort zone: Challenge yourself to try new things and step outside of your comfort zone to inspire creativity and new opportunities.

Surround yourself with inspiration: Create a space that inspires you. Fill it with artwork, motivational quotes, and objects that spark your creativity. Surround yourself with books, movies, and music that encourage you to think differently.

Embrace failure and learn from it: Creativity often comes with a fair share of failures and mistakes. Don't let setbacks discourage you; Embrace the idea that failure is a stepping stone to success and use it to fuel your creativity.

Practice mindfulness and reflection: Take time to slow down and be present in the moment. Engage in activities that promote mindfulness, such as meditation or journaling. Reflect on your thoughts and experiences, allowing for deeper insights and sparking new ideas.

Collaborate with others: Seek opportunities to collaborate with others and bounce ideas off them. Surround yourself with like-minded individuals who share your passion for creativity. They can offer fresh perspectives and bring extra dimensions to your creative process.

Take breaks and recharge: Sometimes, the best way to be more creative is to step away from the task at hand and give yourself a break. Engage in activities that bring you joy and recharge your mind, like walking in nature, listening to music, or simply daydreaming.

Embrace your unique perspective: Recognise that your perspective and experiences are unique to you. Welcome this individuality and use it as a driving force for your creativity. Share your ideas and insights with others, allowing your unique perspective to shine through.

Creativity is not only linked to traditional art forms; you can express it in various ways in all aspects of your life. Your creativity can guide you to new and exciting ventures.

Part five: Improve communication

Improving **communication** refers to boosting exchange of information, thoughts, and ideas between individuals or groups in a more effective and efficient manner.

It involves using various methods, skills, and techniques to ensure clear and concise conveyance of messages, active listening, understanding, and proper interpretation of information.

The goal is to minimise misunderstandings, promote mutual understanding, and establish stronger connections and relationships between people.

Improved communication can lead to increased productivity, enhanced collaboration, better decision-making, and stronger interpersonal bonds.

47. Rapport and Eye contact

Getting into rapport means connecting with another person. Get in tune with them in various ways, such as matching and mirroring their posture and breathing.

Rapport is a term used in psychology and communication to describe a strong and trusting connection between people. It is the foundation for effective communication and understanding. Building rapport is important in therapy, sales, negotiations, and social interactions.

The key to establishing rapport is creating a sense of connection and empathy. You can achieve this by actively listening, mirroring body language, asking open-ended questions, and showing genuine interest and respect.

Active listening means fully focusing on the person, making eye contact, and paying attention.

It also includes reflecting on what the person is saying to show your understanding and encourage further conversation.

Mirroring body language is another effective way to establish rapport. This means subtly mimicking the other person's gestures, posture, and facial expressions. It helps create a sense of empathy and understanding, as it signals that you are on the same wavelength.

Asking open-ended questions encourages others to express their thoughts and feelings. Asking questions that start with "why," "how," or "tell me more" allows for deeper discussions and helps build a connection.

Showing genuine interest and respect is crucial to building rapport. People can sense when someone is being insincere or disinterested. Care about others' thoughts and feelings to build trust and openness.

Rapport is the glue that holds any relationship together. It includes active listening, mirroring body language, asking open-ended questions, and showing genuine interest and respect. By building rapport, you foster better communication, understanding, and long-lasting connections.

There are several components of rapport of which making eye contact is one. You keep contact softly, rather than hard staring, which can feel threatening, so better to look away from time to time, and then make contact again.

Looking into someone's eyes creates a strong bond. It is a simple yet effective way to show respect, engagement, and interest in the person you are communicating with. Whether you are having a conversation, giving a presentation, or meeting someone new, making eye contact is an essential skill to master.

Maintain a natural and comfortable gaze. Avoid staring too intensely, as this can be off-putting and make the other person feel uncomfortable. Instead, allow your eyes to meet theirs briefly before breaking eye contact momentarily. This will help create a rhythm and flow to the conversation.

Be mindful of cultural and personal differences. In some cultures, direct eye contact may be seen as a sign of respect, while in others, it may be considered impolite or intrusive. It's important to adapt to cultural differences when interacting with people from diverse cultures.

Maintaining eye contact while someone is speaking, shows that you are fully present and actively listening. It conveys that their words are important to you and that you genuinely care about what they are saying. Eye contact plays a significant role in listening and understanding. Looking into someone's eyes helps you understand their emotions and intentions.

Making eye contact can be challenging. Some individuals may feel nervous or uncomfortable when looking into someone's eyes. Practice increasing eye contact gradually with close friends or family members in relaxed situations. With time and practice, you can overcome the discomfort and make eye contact more naturally.

Making eye contact is a crucial aspect of effective communication. It helps establish a connection, shows respect and interest, and enhances understanding. By mastering this skill, you can improve your relationships. Next time you find yourself in a conversation, remember the importance of making eye contact and let your eyes do the talking.

48. Mirror and match.

Mirror: Pay attention to the other person's body language and mirror their posture and movements for better connection. The important thing is to do this subtly. It is a powerful tool that reveals your thoughts, your actions, and the choices you make. Just like a physical mirror, life reflects your beauty, flaws, and imperfections. It is a constant reminder that what you see in others is often a reflection of yourself.

Match: Life is not just about finding a perfect match; it is also about challenging yourself and growing beyond your comfort zone. Sometimes, life throws you into situations that feel mismatched, forcing you to confront your fears and limitations. These mismatches test your patience and adaptability. They encourage you to broaden your perspectives and explore new possibilities.

The mirror and match of life work together and offer contrast to help us appreciate the beauty of both harmony and contrast. The mirror reflects our true selves, encouraging self-reflection and introspection. It helps us recognise our patterns, beliefs, and behaviours that need improvement or celebration.

Life's mirrors and matches teach valuable lessons. They remind you to appreciate the beauty and uniqueness of everyone you encounter. They guide you towards self-improvement, authenticity, and embracing the diversity of experiences. Both mirror and match are essential elements that shape your perception of life.

49. Open body language.

————

Open body language refers to the way you carry yourself and the non-verbal cues you give off that show you are approachable and willing to engage with others. It involves both your physical posture and your facial expressions. These have a significant impact on the impressions you make and the connections you form with others.

When your body language is open, you have an upright and relaxed posture. You avoid crossing your arms or legs, as this can create a barrier between you and others. Your shoulders are back, and you hold your head high. This posture conveys confidence and openness, making others feel comfortable approaching you.

Your facial expression plays a critical role in conveying openness. A genuine smile can go a long way in showing friendliness and approachability. Eye contact is also essential, as it shows interest and attentiveness in the person you are interacting with.

Open body language can have a positive impact on your interactions with others in various settings. Building rapport and trust in professional settings can improve communication and collaboration.

Being approachable and friendly in social settings helps you connect with others and build meaningful relationships.

Open body language should be genuine and authentic. Trying to mimic open body language without genuinely feeling open can come across as insincere. It is essential to cultivate a sense of warmth and openness within yourself first, which will naturally reflect in your body language.

Open body language is a powerful tool that can enhance your interactions. Paying attention to how you hold yourself and your facial expressions promotes open connections with others.

50. Speak Clearly.

Speaking clearly means saying precisely what you want to convey. Lack of understanding and poor communication may be because you are not using simple words or not pronouncing words carefully.

Speaking clearly is an important skill that can help you communicate effectively and be understood by others. Here are some tips to improve your clarity of speech:

Slow down: One of the most common reasons for unclear speech is speaking too quickly. Take your time and pause between sentences or ideas to allow others to absorb what you're saying.

Pronounce words clearly: Pay attention to each word and enunciate them clearly. Avoid mumbling or slurring your words. Practice saying each sound clearly.

Use proper pronunciation: Take the time to learn the correct pronunciation of words, especially those that are frequently used in your conversations. Use dictionaries or online resources to ensure accuracy.

Use pauses and emphasis: Use pauses and emphasis to highlight key points. This can help make your speech more engaging and easier for others to understand.

Monitor your breathing: Adequate breath control is essential for clear speech. Breathe deeply from your diaphragm and avoid shallow breathing that can cause your words to flow together.

Avoid filler words: Filler words, such as "um" or "uh," can make your speech sound less clear and confident. Practice eliminating these fillers by pausing or using transitional phrases instead.

Practice active listening: Pay attention to other people's speech patterns, vocal clarity, and pronunciation. By listening carefully, you can learn from others and improve your own communication skills.

Seek feedback: Ask friends, family, or colleagues to provide constructive feedback on your clarity of speech. They may identify areas for improvement or suggest exercises to help you improve.

Practice regularly: Like any skill, coherent speech improves with practice. Engage in regular conversations, and public speaking, or join speaking clubs to refine your ability to articulate.

Clarity of speech requires practice and conscious effort. Use these tips and techniques to improve your speaking skills and make communication easier for everyone.

51. Be positive.

Start with a positive statement before making a complaint or request. People are more likely to respond positively when they feel appreciated.

Being positive is a powerful mindset that can have a transformative impact on your life. It is a choice you can make every day, regardless of the circumstances you find yourself in. Here are a few reasons being positive is so important:

Improved mental well-being: When you choose to focus on the positive aspects of your life, you train your mind to see the good in every situation. This can lead to reduced stress, anxiety, and depression, as you shift your perspective to a more optimistic outlook.

Increased resilience: Positive people are better equipped to handle challenges and setbacks. They have a greater ability to bounce back from adversity, as they believe in their capacity to overcome obstacles and find solutions. Being positive helps you handle challenges with strength.

Enhanced relationships: Positive individuals attract and maintain healthier relationships. Their positive attitude and energy to create a better environment for everyone. By radiating positivity, you can make a positive impact on others, inspiring them to embrace a more optimistic mindset as well.

Improved physical health: Several studies have shown that positive thinking can have a beneficial effect on our physical health. Positive people have less stress, stronger immune systems, and lower risk of certain illnesses. By being positive, you can nurture your overall well-being and improve your physical health.

Increased productivity and success: Positive individuals are more likely to set goals, act, and persevere, which can lead to greater success.

A belief in their abilities and a positive vision for the future motivated them. You can unlock your full potential and achieve your goals in both personal and professional endeavours.

Being positive is a powerful choice that can transform your life in multiple ways. Having a positive outlook can improve your mental and physical health, relationships, and success. Embrace positivity and create a brighter and more fulfilling future for yourself and those around you.

52. End a discussion positively.

Close your conversation with a positive statement, as they will remember it over the negativity. Here are examples of some ways to end a conversation positively:

- In conclusion, the topic we discussed has presented various challenges and complexities. However, it is important to remember that even in the face of these challenges, there is always room for hope and positive change.
- By applying these ideas and working together, we can create a brighter future for ourselves and future generations.
- Engaging in open and respectful discussions like the one we have had today is crucial. It allows us to share different perspectives and find common ground. Through such discussions, we broaden our understanding and collectively move towards finding sustainable solutions.
- It is essential to recognise that change takes time and effort. It requires continuous learning, adaptability, and collaboration. By working together with a positive attitude and determination, you can make remarkable progress.
- By focusing on the possibilities, we can ignite a sense of optimism and create a ripple effect of positive change in our communities and beyond.
- In the end, it is our collective commitment to making a difference. Each one of us has the power to contribute, no matter how small our actions may seem. Together, we can shape a world that is more inclusive, sustainable, and compassionate.
- Let us leave this discussion with a renewed sense of hope and

a deep-seated belief in our ability to create a better tomorrow. By working together, our positive impact can be far-reaching and transformative.

53. Concentrate.

———

Concentrate. As you sit in a quiet space, let your mind be in the present moment. Take a deep breath and feel the air fill your lungs. Focus on the sensation of each inhale and exhale, allowing your breath to become your anchor in the present.

Now, shift your attention to your body. Feel the weight of your body on the surface you're sitting or lying on. Notice any areas of tension or discomfort and consciously release them. Relax your muscles, starting from your toes and working your way up to the top of your head. Feel a sense of ease and relaxation spreading throughout your body.

Next, bring your attention to your thoughts. Let them come and go without judgment, like passing cars on a road. Allow any worries or stressful thoughts to float away as you focus solely on this moment. Feel a sense of clarity and calmness as your mind becomes free from distractions.

Now, turn your attention to your senses. What do you see around you? Take in the colours, shapes, and textures of your surroundings. Notice any sounds you can hear, both near and far. Take a moment to savour any tastes or smells that may be present in your environment.

As you bring your focus back to your breath, notice how it is steady and rhythmic. Feel the gentle rise and fall of your chest with each inhale and exhale. Allow your breath to guide you deeper into a state of concentration.

With each breath, let go of any thoughts, worries, or distractions that arise. Keep your focus solely on your breath, allowing it to bring you into a state of flow and presence. Imagine your mind becoming clear and uncluttered, ready to fully engage with the task or activity that lies ahead.

Take a few more moments to sit in this state of concentration, enjoying the sense of calm and focus that it brings. When you're ready, slowly bring your awareness back to the present moment, feeling refreshed and centred.

Concentration is a skill that improves with practice. Adding moments of focus to your daily routine can improve clarity and help in all aspects of life.

54. Communicate clearly.

Make sure others understand what you are asking them to do because they may not have heard you properly. They may have heard the start of what you were saying and then go into their own assumptions about what you were asking them.

When aiming to communicate clearly, there are a few key things to keep in mind:

Be concise: Avoid using excessive jargon or technical language that may confuse your audience. Instead, use clear language to relay your message effectively.

Organise your thoughts: Structure your communication logically. Start with an introduction that states the main point, then provide supporting details, and end with a logical conclusion.

Use visual aids when necessary: Use visual aids like charts or graphs to explain complex information.

Check for understanding: To ensure your message is being understood, periodically check in with your audience. Ask if anyone has questions or needs clarification on any specific points. This will help you address any misunderstandings in real time.

Be aware of non-verbal cues: Communication is not just about words, but also about body language, tone of voice, and facial expressions. Pay attention to these non-verbal cues and make sure they align with the message you are trying to convey.

Active listening: When engaging in a conversation, give your undivided attention to the person speaking. Focus on what they are saying, ask clarifying questions, and show empathy and understanding. This will help establish a clearer and more effective line of communication.

Effective communication requires practice and an understanding of your audience. Practising these strategies and understanding your audience improves your ability to communicate clearly. This ensures that others receive and understand your message.

55. Summarise.

———

At the end of a conversation, sum up your discussion because it's easy to remember the end of a discussion and forget the beginning of it. Summarise by saying this is what we discussed, and this is what will happen now.

A summary is a brief and condensed representation of the main points or ideas expressed in a text, speech, or any other form of communication. The aim is to present crucial information concisely, enabling readers to grasp the main points without reading the entire article.

To create a summary, you must carefully analyse the material and identify the principal arguments, themes, or events. It involves extracting the most important information and discarding unnecessary details or supporting examples. You should also write the summary in your own words while retaining the original meaning.

Summaries are useful tools for various purposes, such as studying, research, and decision-making. They enable readers to assess whether a piece of content is relevant or interesting to them. They provide a structured overview that aids comprehension.

Summaries provide a snapshot of the essential information, saving time and effort for those seeking a quick understanding of a topic.

56. Use your body to communicate.

Use your body along with your voice. Adopt a strong, relaxed, open posture like in martial arts: legs slightly apart, knees bent.

Using your body to communicate is an innate and powerful form of expression. Nonverbal cues like posture, gestures, and facial expressions can convey emotions and meaning. Here are ways to use your body to communicate:

Your posture communicates your confidence, mood, and level of engagement. Having good posture, with an open chest, can show confidence and approachability. Slouching may show a lack of interest or low energy. By being mindful of your posture, you can ensure that your body communicates your intentions accurately.

Eye contact: they often refer eyes to as the windows to the soul. Making eye contact with someone shows them you are attentive to what they have to say. It also helps in building trust and creating a stronger connection during conversations.

Facial expressions are incredibly expressive and can effectively convey your emotions. Smiling shows happiness or friendliness while frowning suggests displeasure or concern. By being aware of your facial expressions, you can ensure that it accurately communicates your emotions to others.

Gestures can enhance the message you want to convey. For example, pointing can show direction, while waving can serve as a greeting or farewell. It's important to be aware of cultural differences, as gestures might have different meanings in various cultures.

Body movements can convey meaning and add depth to your communication. Nodding subtly means agreement or understanding while shaking your head means disagreement or disbelief. Leaning forward shows interest, while leaning back may show disengagement or scepticism.

Physical touch, such as a handshake, hug, or pat on the back, can communicate warmth, comfort, and support. However, it's important to be mindful of personal boundaries and cultural norms when using touch as communication.

Personal space between individuals can communicate levels of intimacy or formality. Standing too close to someone can make them uncomfortable while standing too far away can create distance. Adjusting your proximity can help create a more comfortable and meaningful interaction.

Effective communication involves more than just words. Utilising your body to communicate can enhance understanding, strengthen relationships, and foster a deeper connection with others. So, use this powerful tool and express yourself not only with words but through your entire being.

57. Be confident.

————

Develop the confidence and self-belief that you may do or not do what it is you want, so long as you are not causing harm to others by so doing.

Confidence is a quality that can transform your life, both personally and professionally. Confidence attracts others and helps you overcome challenges. Here are ways to help you become more confident:

Positive self-talk: Pay attention to the thoughts that run through your mind. Replace negative and self-doubting thoughts with positive affirmations and belief in your abilities. Remind yourself of your strengths and past successes.

Failure is a natural part of life and does not define you. Instead of dwelling on mistakes and setbacks, view them as learning opportunities that contribute to your growth. Embracing failures helps you develop resilience and adaptability, which ultimately boosts your confidence.

Practice self-care: Taking care of yourself physically, mentally, and emotionally is essential for building confidence. Make time for activities that bring you joy and relaxation. Exercise regularly, eat well, and get enough sleep. When you feel good about yourself, your confidence soars.

Set achievable goals: Break down larger goals into smaller, manageable tasks. Each minor success builds your confidence and belief in your ability to achieve larger goals. Celebrate your successes along the way, no matter how small they may seem.

Your body language speaks volumes about your confidence. Stand tall, maintain eye contact, and use assertive yet friendly gestures when communicating with others. Adopting a powerful pose or a confident walk can instantly boost your self-assurance.

Surrounding yourself with positive influences can boost your confidence. Seek mentors, friends, or colleagues who inspire you and provide constructive feedback. Their belief in you will reinforce your self-belief.

Take advantage of opportunities for growth to invest in yourself. Read books, attend workshops, take courses, or acquire new skills that align with your goals. Expanding your knowledge and expertise will instil confidence in your abilities.

Take risks: Stepping outside your comfort zone is crucial for personal growth and confidence-building. Challenge yourself to take calculated risks and try new things. Even if you face failure, you'll gain experience and confidence in your ability to handle different situations.

Building confidence is an ongoing process that requires patience and self-reflection. Celebrate your progress and be kind to yourself during setbacks. Believe in yourself, embrace your strengths, and live a successful life.

58. State clearly what you want.

Be direct about your wants or expectations without making excuses or giving too many reasons, as it can confuse the other person. Clarify a few things to ensure he or she plainly understands what needs to be done.

Provide details about the specific objectives and desired outcome of the task. Let them know what the result should look like, as well as any key elements or requirements that need to be considered.

Provide a timeline or deadline for the task. Having a clear timeframe will allow them to plan accordingly and organise their workload.

To state clearly what you want, follow these steps:

Identify your objective: Clearly understand what it is that you want. Is it a tangible item, a specific action, or a desired outcome?

Be specific: Avoid vague or ambiguous language. Clearly articulate your request with specific details, such as the type, quantity, quality, or timeframe related to your objective.

Use simple language: Keep your statement concise and easy to understand. Avoid unnecessary jargon or complex terms that may confuse the listener.

Use "I" statements making your request from your perspective. This helps convey ownership and responsibility for your wants. Instead of saying, "You should do this," say, "I would like..."

Be assertive, not aggressive: While it's important to be clear and direct, it's equally important to maintain a respectful tone. Avoid sounding demanding or aggressive, as this can create a negative response.

Consider the recipient's perspective: Think about how your request might be received by the person or group you are communicating with. Tailor your language to make it more likely they will understand and respond positively.

Provide reasons, if possible: If there are specific reasons behind your request, consider briefly explaining them. This can help the recipient understand your needs and may increase the likelihood of a positive response.

Practice active listening: After stating your request, actively listen to the response. This allows you to confirm mutual understanding and address any questions or concerns. Effective communication involves a dialogue and a willingness to clarify if necessary.

Follow up, if needed: If the response or action you received does not align with what you want, follow up to clarify and restate your request. Persistence can be key in ensuring your request is understood and fulfilled.

Clear communication is essential in getting what you want. By being specific, using simple language, and considering the recipient's perspective, you can increase the chances of your request being clearly understood and successfully met.

59. Don't accuse others.

———

Don't say 'You make me cross' or similar. Instead, acknowledge your emotions by saying 'When you do that, I feel cross'.

Accusations can have long-lasting consequences, both personally and professionally. It is crucial to approach any potential conflict with an open mind and a willingness to understand each side of the story. When you accuse others without valid proof, you risk hurting their reputation and causing them distress.

Instead of jumping to conclusions or making assumptions, it is better to engage in open dialogue. Communication is often the key to resolving conflicts and misunderstandings. Talking calmly can dispel doubts and clear up any misunderstandings.

Nobody is perfect. Everyone makes mistakes, and sometimes it is easy to misinterpret someone's intentions or actions. Instead of pointing fingers and placing blame, focus on seeking understanding and finding a resolution.

If accusations seem necessary, it is advisable to approach the matter in a sensitive and considerate manner. Gather concrete evidence, speak to all the involved parties, and ensure transparency. It is essential to maintain fairness, respect, and a dedication to the truth when trying to address and resolve any issues.

Don't accuse others without valid evidence or proper justification. It is important to consider different perspectives and gather all the facts before making any allegations.

Accusing someone prematurely can harm relationships and create unnecessary tension. Instead, approach conflicts with an open mind, engage in dialogue, and seek to understand different perspectives. Keep fairness and respect in mind, relying on facts rather than assumptions to reach a resolution.

60. Listen.

It's easy to become overwhelmed. The chatter of people and the buzzing of technology can feel like an unending cacophony. But amidst all the noise, there are moments of clarity and beauty waiting to be discovered, if only we listen carefully. Wait for a response instead of assuming someone's agreement or refusal.

Take a moment to close your eyes and tune in to the world around you. Breathe in deeply and let your senses awaken. Focus on the sounds that may go unnoticed in the rush of everyday life.

Listen to the sounds of nature: the chirping of birds, the rustling of leaves, the gentle flow of a nearby stream. Let their sweet melodies soothe your soul and remind you of the interconnectedness of all living beings.

Listen to the voices of loved ones: the laughter of children, the comforting tone of a friend's advice, the loving whispers of a partner. These simple sounds hold immeasurable value and can bring warmth and joy to the heart.

Listen to the wisdom within yourself: the quiet voice that speaks in moments of reflection and solitude. Trust your intuition and let it guide you towards the paths that are right for you.

Listen to strangers: their hopes, dreams, and fears. By listening to others' stories, we can create a world of kindness and compassion.

Listen to the lessons that life is teaching you. Every experience, both joyful and challenging, offers an opportunity for growth. By paying attention and being open to the surrounding messages, you can learn valuable insights that will shape your journey.

Listen carefully to the world around you. Be present and attuned to the sounds that are waiting to be discovered. Embrace the power of listening, for it can bring you closer to the essence of life itself.

61. Don't make assumptions.

Assumptions can lead to misunderstandings, false beliefs, and miscommunication. They are based on limited information or personal biases and can prevent you from understanding the full picture or truth of a situation.

If you make assumptions, you are making up a story in your mind without having all the facts. This can be harmful in relationships, both personal and professional, as it can create unnecessary conflict and tension.

Instead of making assumptions, try to gather all the relevant information and ask clarifying questions if needed. Communicate openly and honestly with others to ensure that you agree and clearly understand the situation.

Everyone has their unique perspective, experiences, and beliefs. Making assumptions about others can be unfair and can lead to judgment and prejudice. Allow space for different viewpoints and try to approach situations with an open mind.

By avoiding assumptions, you can promote understanding, empathy, and effective communication. Building stronger relationships helps create an inclusive and harmonious environment for all.

Be mindful of your assumptions and actively challenge them. To grow and maintain good relationships, seek understanding, and communicate openly without making assumptions.

62. Use the stuck record technique.

The stuck record technique is a method of repetition and persistence that can persuade or negotiate in difficult situations. It involves repeating a specific statement or question repeatedly, like a stuck record, until you compel the other person to listen or respond.

Here is an example of how you can use the stuck record technique.

You are in a meeting with your colleagues, and you are supporting a change in a company policy. However, your colleagues are not convinced and seem to brush off your suggestion. In this situation, you can use the stuck record technique to make your point heard.

State your point concisely and assertively: Begin by clearly stating your suggestion or argument. For example, "I believe changing this policy will improve our department's efficiency."

Repeat your statement: Regardless of what others say or how they respond, continue to repeat your initial statement. You could say, "I understand your concerns, but I still think changing this policy will make our department more efficient."

Stay calm and composed during the conversation, even if it gets tough. This will help you appear more confident and increase the effectiveness of the stuck record technique.

Stick to your point and don't let others divert the conversation. This repetition is key to making your point memorable and difficult to ignore.

Listen actively: While you are repeating your argument, listen to the responses of others. This will allow you to address their concerns directly and tailor your response accordingly.

You will break through resistance by using the stuck record technique. You want to guide the conversation towards finding common ground or a compromise that benefits everyone involved.

Use the stuck record technique with caution. Overusing this technique can come across as aggressive or confrontational, so it's important to gauge the dynamics of the conversation and adjust your approach accordingly.

63. Learn to say 'no.'

I f you don't want to do something, just say 'no.' Don't give lots of reasons because whatever you say it is likely that you will be offered a way to solve that problem meaning that you would then say 'yes' instead of 'no.'

Learning to say 'no' is an important skill that can help you maintain your boundaries, prioritise your own needs, and manage your time effectively. Saying 'no' might feel uncomfortable at first, but with practice, you can learn to say it assertively yet respectfully. Here are some tips to learn how to say 'no':

Understand your own priorities: Before you can say 'no' to others, you need to know what your priorities and limits are. Take some time to figure out what is important to you and what commitments you can realistically take on.

Be direct and firm: When you decide to say 'no', do so clearly and assertively. Avoid being wishy-washy or overly apologetic, as this can leave room for negotiation or guilt-tripping. Be confident in your decision and address it.

Offer alternatives when possible: If you genuinely want to help but can not say 'yes' to a request, offer alternatives. Suggest someone else who may assist or propose a different timeframe that works better for you. This shows your willingness to find a solution without sacrificing your own needs.

Give yourself permission: Remind yourself that it is okay to say 'no.' You may set boundaries and prioritise your own well-being. Recognise that saying 'yes' to everything can lead to burnout and resentment, so it is important to take care of yourself first.

Practice saying 'no': Saying 'no' can be difficult if you are not used to asserting yourself in such situations. Practice saying 'no' in front of a mirror or with a trusted friend or family member. This will help you feel more comfortable and confident when the situation arises.

Use 'I' statements: When declining a request, use 'I' statements to express your needs and boundaries. For example, saying, "I'm sorry, but I can't take on any additional projects right now" is more effective than saying, "You're asking too much of me."

Stay considerate and respectful: While it is important to say 'no', it is equally important to be respectful and considerate towards the other person's feelings. Express your appreciation for their consideration and explain your circumstances honestly. You are declining the request, not the person. Learning to say 'no' is an ongoing process.

64. Don't blame others.

Refrain from mocking the other person's character with negative accusations. Each person's perspective is unique, so mentioning your plans may provoke envy or remorse in them. Adding insult to injury is unnecessary in such situations.

It's easy to point fingers and place blame on others when things don't go as planned. It's human nature to want to shift the responsibility onto someone else, to avoid feeling guilty or facing consequences. But blaming others for your failures or mistakes is not a productive or fair approach.

Blaming others robs you of the opportunity for self-growth and personal development. When you refuse to take accountability for your actions, you become stagnant in your own life. You can improve and become a better version of yourself by taking responsibility for your choices and learning from your mistakes.

Blaming others creates a toxic and negative environment. It erodes trust and damages relationships. When you point fingers at others, it becomes difficult to build strong, supportive connections. People don't want to be around someone who plays the blame game. They want to be around someone who takes ownership of their actions and works towards finding solutions.

Blaming others lacks empathy and understanding. It cannot recognise that everyone makes mistakes and has flaws. By being compassionate and empathetic, you can foster a culture of understanding and forgiveness. Instead of blaming others, you can choose to support and uplift each other, recognising that you are all doing your best.

Blaming others is not productive. It shifts the focus away from problem-solving and finding solutions. Instead of wasting time and energy on assigning blame, focus on identifying the root cause of the issue and work together to rectify it. By focusing on finding solutions, you increase the chances of positive results and a harmonious environment.

Resist the temptation to blame others for your failures or mistakes. Taking responsibility for your actions helps with personal growth, building relationships, showing empathy, and problem-solving. Instead of pointing fingers, focus on personal accountability and work towards building a better future.

65. Believe in yourself.

Above all else, **believe in yourself** and your ability to achieve many things, even when others shake their heads and tell you it's a challenge. Find out what you must learn and do it if it's something you want to do.

Believe in yourself. These words hold immense power and potential. They are the foundation upon which you build dreams, achieve success, and overcome hurdles. In a world filled with doubts and insecurities, it is crucial to remind yourself of your inherent worth and capabilities.

No one knows you better than yourself. You possess a unique set of skills, talents, and perspectives that no one else can replicate. Embrace this individuality and understand that you have something valuable to offer to the world.

Believing in yourself is easier said than done. It requires an unwavering faith in your abilities, even and especially in the face of adversity. It means looking past your weaknesses and focusing on your strengths. It means cultivating self-confidence and a positive mindset.

It is natural to question yourself and your abilities. Doubts can creep in, making you second-guess your decisions and capabilities. But it is during these moments that believing in yourself becomes crucial. It is in these moments that you must remind yourself of your past achievements, no matter how small they may seem.

Believing in yourself means embracing failure as a stepping stone to success. Mistakes and setbacks are inevitable parts of life, but they do not define you. Instead, they provide valuable lessons and opportunities for growth. By believing in yourself, you can dust yourself off, learn from your failures, and come back even stronger.

Surrounding yourself with supportive and encouraging people is equally important. Seek those who believe in you, and who see your potential. Fuel your self-belief. Surrounding yourself with positivity can help drown out the negative voices, both internal and external, that may try to tear you down.

Success rarely comes easily or quickly. It requires hard work, dedication, and perseverance. But by believing in yourself, you are already one step ahead. With self-belief, the impossible becomes possible, and dreams become realities.

Embrace your strengths, acknowledge your weaknesses, and believe in yourself. With self-belief as your driving force, there is no limit to what you can achieve.

66. FINALLY

I wrote this book because there have been times when I've wanted to make major or minor changes to my life, yet I have felt stuck about how to bring those changes about.

I didn't believe I could make the changes I wanted to make. I worried about others' opinions, so I procrastinated because:

- Change seemed unachievable.
- I didn't know how to start.
- I wanted other people to change.
- I didn't have enough time.
- I was scared to take the first step.

However, I learned that simple steps could enable me to make the changes I wanted.

I hope you find the suggestions in this book useful and will take action to change your life by following whatever steps are relevant to your situation.

Just like a spreadsheet – when you change one thing everything else changes!

You really can change your life!

About the Author

If you enjoyed this book, please take a moment to leave a review on the website from which you downloaded or bought this book.

Reviews are so important for independent authors. Thank you very much.

I live by the sea in Cornwall, UK. I've written personal development and self-help books for doctors and others, books about retirement and novels.

I was a doctor for thirty years and then did something else. After attending a workshop based on Louise Hay's book 'You Can Heal Your Life', I trained to be a Louise Hay workshop leader. I did this in 1999 in San Diego and for several years ran workshops in Cornwall, UK. These workshops aimed to enable participants to understand themselves better and then find how to move forward more positively in life.

I read an article about Coaching, so I trained with CoachU, In 2000. I realised that as a doctor, I had useful and special insights and life experience about what life is like as a doctor, so I focussed on coaching doctors.

I wrote an article called 'Is there life after Medicine?' for the BMJ hoping that it would be published in 'Personal View.' However even though the panel rejected it I was contacted by and later met Rhona MacDonald, the editor of Career Focus, part of the British Medical Journal. She was very interested in what I was doing and encouraged me to write a series of articles about Life Coaching and how it can enable doctors to have a life. As a result, I wrote each month about how doctors could have more time and better work-life balance. These articles were published in the British Medical Journal over the years 2000-2005 and eventually evolved into books for doctors: 'Prescription for Change - for Doctors Who Want a life' and 'ABC of Change for Doctors.' 'Life after Medicine - for Doctors who Want a Trouble-free Transition' was published later.

Since then, I've also written and published various books, eBooks and audiobooks: personal development books for doctors, self-help books, and novels.

Now retired from Coaching, I'm updating my books and writing more.

Read more at https://susankersley.co.uk[1]

---

1. https://susankersley.co.uk/

Don't miss out!

Visit the website below and you can sign up to receive emails whenever Susan Kersley publishes a new book. There's no charge and no obligation.

https://books2read.com/r/B-A-EFNC-ADURC

BOOKS 2 READ

Connecting independent readers to independent writers.

Did you love *How to Change Your Life*? Then you should read *How to Have a Balanced Life*[2] by Susan Kersley!

Chaotic life? Never get much done? Want more balance?

Simple changes can give you big results.

Are you neglecting important aspects of your life because you don't have enough balance? Do you struggle to achieve what you want?

Let Susan Kersley guide you through simple steps to reach your goals, find more balance and rediscover forgotten parts of yourself.

The author is a retired medical doctor and was a life coach for fifteen years.

How to have a balanced life is a well written, concise personal development book with easy to follow suggestions that will make a big

---

2. https://books2read.com/u/brlLzm

3. https://books2read.com/u/brlLzm

difference to your life. You'll find simple changes you can make today and discover how these will have a rapid positive impact on your life.

Buy the book today and find your way to peace and personal stability.

Read more at https://susankersley.co.uk.

Also by Susan Kersley

A Novel
Pills and Pillboxes
Connection Deception

Books about Weight Management
Change Your Mind, Change Your Weight
Mind Over Weight
Weight Loss Success

Books for Doctors
ABC of Change for Doctors
Life After Medicine
Prescription for Change
Work-Life Balance for Doctors
Lifestyle Coaching for Doctors
Meet the Challenges of Working as a Doctor
The Busy Doctor's Guide: Improve your Work-Life Balance

Retirement Books
Get Ready for Retirement
Life After Work
Retirement: Back to Basics

Self-help Books
How to Have a Balanced Life
69 Easy Ways to Change Your life
15 Ways to Change Your Life
Connect and Change
Coping With New Year Resolutions
More Time for You Now
How to Change Your Life

Watch for more at https://susankersley.co.uk.

www.ingramcontent.com/pod-product-compliance
Lightning Source LLC
Chambersburg PA
CBHW020240160726
47987CB00019B/439